A.G. NOORANI

THE RSS AND THE BJP
A DIVISION OF LABOUR

Other titles in the series

First published December 2000
Reprinted, with updated Epilogue, March 2001
LeftWord Books
12 Rajendra Prasad Road
New Delhi 110 001
INDIA
Phone: (91-11) 335 9456, 335 6966
Email: leftword@vsnl.com

LeftWord Books is a division of
Naya Rasta Publishers Pvt. Ltd.
27–29 Bhai Vir Singh Marg
New Delhi 110 001
India

ISBN 81-87496-13-4

Typeset in Garamond and BankGothic

Printed at Progressive Printers
A 21 Jhilmil Industrial Area
Grand Trunk Road
Shahdara
Delhi 110 095
India

To the memory of
JAWAHARLAL NEHRU

CONTENTS

Acknowledgements

All quotes in the following chapters are from contemporary newspapers and magazines, unless otherwise stated. Wherever emphasis appears in quotes, it is as a rule added by the present author. Much of the material presented here has appeared in my articles published in *The Statesman*, *Frontline*, and *Imprint* (in 1984) over the last decade or more. I wish to thank the editors of all these publications. None of them, of course, is responsible for the contents of this book. To no small extent the publication of this book is due to the pains which Sudhanva Deshpande, Managing Editor, LeftWord Books took so cheerfully.

ABBREVIATIONS

AA	*Asian Age*
CC	*Communalism Combat*
EPW	*Economic and Political Weekly*
ET	*Economic Times*
HT	*The Hindustan Times*
IE	*Indian Express*
SO	*Sunday Observer*
TH	*The Hindu*
TOI	*The Times of India*
TS	*The Statesman*
TT	*The Telegraph*

PREFACE

A strikingly consistent feature of the Rashtriya Swayamsevak Sangh's (RSS) style, which its political arm, the Jan Sangh, and its successor the Bharatiya Janata Party (BJP), emulated, is calculated ambiguity. They are innately communal, but intensely resent the charge and claim to be 'nationalists'. They would avow that in their political lexicon 'Hindu' covers all who are born in Hindustan. In definitive pronouncements and policies, however, it is Hindus as 'the majority community', harassed by the very 'minorities' (read: Muslims and Christians) whom they had 'appeased'. A new front was opened in 2000; more precisely, reopened. Its target, incredibly, are the Sikhs. The new supremo of the RSS, Kuppahali Seetaramaiyah Sudarshan, led the Quixotic charge, no sooner he had mounted the steed, only to invite in response at Chandigarh invective that, happily, is rare in our political discourse.

Sudarshan is a professed hardliner. Bangaru Laxman, house-trained to speak softly, was elected, rather appointed, as BJP's President, not long after Sudarshan's elevation. And he was anointed with the RSS's blessings. The media went into a spin trying to understand exactly what was afoot. As swiftly as Sudarshan espoused the hard line, Bangaru Laxman began wooing Muslims, albeit pretentiously. The performance was meant for a different audience, though. It is the millions of Hindus who have always rejected the politics of hate practised by the Hindu Mahasabha of V.D. Savarkar and Shyama Prasad Mookerjee and of the RSS and the fronts it established. The Jan Sangh was founded by Mookerjee in 1951 under a pact with the RSS's chieftain M.S. Golwalkar. The RSS lent the muscle and ensured its control.

The French scholar Christophe Jaffrelot, describing the events of 1989 when, on the eve of elections to the Lok Sabha, the BJP took up the Ayodhya issue in its famous Palampur resolution, has described the *parivar's* recourse to calculated ambiguity: 'A division of labour then took place between Advani and Vajpayee who presented a more moderate face of Hindu nationalism.'[1] The language used in the resolution was characteristically ambiguous. It demanded that the site of the Babri Masjid be 'handed over to the Hindus'. It left unsaid what the BJP would do to the mosque that stood on the site. That was revealed on December 6, 1992.

On one point, however, the resolution shed ambiguity. That was when it spoke, revealingly, of 'the sentiments of the overwhelming majority in this country – the Hindus.' Advani has acknowledged with unconcealed pride the dividends which this plank in the election campaign yielded to the BJP. This party has come to power after it had plunged the country into turmoil and its President, L.K. Advani, had waded through the blood of his fellow country-men during his *rath yatra* of 1990.

Amidst all this, ambiguity was practised skillfully and division of labour maintained throughout in the RSS family, the Sangh *parivar* – between the RSS and the BJP; the BJP and the VHP; the BJP and the Bajrang Dal, and of course, Advani and Vajpayee. Individual styles differ; but Vajpayee has never made any secret of the fact that, as he put it, 'the Sangh is my soul.' Temperamentally his preference is for conciliation. His commitment to the shared goal is never in doubt. Vajpayee is an authentic product of the RSS and shares its outlook. Those who expect better of him – and repeatedly court disappointment – would do well to remember the constitutional lawyer, A.V. Dicey's words:

People sometimes ask the idle question why the Pope does not introduce this or that reform? The true answer is that a revolutionist is not the kind of man who becomes a Pope, and that the man who becomes a Pope has no wish to be a revolutionist. Louis the Fourteenth could not in all probability have established Protestantism as the national religion of France; but to imagine Louis the Fourteenth as wishing to carry out a Protestant reformation is nothing short of imagining him to have been a being quite unlike the *Grand Monarque*.[2]

What succour has Vajpayee provided to the beleaguered Christians except words and more words all this time, from March 1998 to September 2000?

The deceit and gore now work no longer. The mosque is demolished and, with it, the BJP's respectability – if it had any to begin with – as well. Hindu militancy can no longer be whipped up as before. The BJP is now faced with the vastly more difficult task of breaking out of its stagnation, by winning the confidence of those very people who reject its outlook and ethos. It has to manage allies, many of whom are unprincipled and wavering. It has to tackle the problems of governance. Yet, it cannot cut the umbilical cord that ties it to the RSS. The RSS very much wants to see the BJP in power, but it cannot pay the price of ideological change or erosion. This is not a 'creative tension'. It is a process of corrosion and decline. Either the Sangh *parivar* (family) will have to be contained and defeated, or Indian secularism, already enfeebled, will have to be abandoned and, with it, democracy as well.

No one foresaw this menace more clearly than Jawaharlal Nehru. His greatness should not be measured by those who profess to love him and use his name; we must judge him, rather, by the kind who hate his memory – the purveyors of communal hate and strife, the Sangh *parivar*. Unlike others, Jawaharlal Nehru was not content merely to sit on the sidelines and watch this fascist movement. He gave battle and fought it all his life so that the secular ideal can survive. It is of such that the poet wrote:

Mahroome haqiqat hain, sahil ke tamashahi
Hum doob ke dekhen hai, daryaon ki gehrai

(They are ignorant of the realities who watch playfully from the river banks / I have plunged deep into the waters to fathom the depths.)

To his memory, this modest work is respectfully dedicated.

Mumbai   A.G. NOORANI
September 16, 2000

1

INTRODUCTION

No event since the defeat of Hitler's fascist regime in 1945 has shaken Europe as much as the entry into Austria's new coalition government on February 4, 2000 of Jorg Haider's Austrian Freedom Party, 'a party with Nazi echoes' as *The Economist* described it. The mainstream conservatives of the Austrian Peoples' Party, led by Wolfgang Schuessel had signed a formal pact with the Freedom Party in order to form a government. It matters little that, as part of the deal, Haider stayed out of the government at the national level. He continues to be the Governor of Corinthian, where his party won the elections last year. His calculations are obvious. Having won respectability, he can become Austria's Chancellor next time. If Europe is disturbed, it is because never since the war has 'a politician widely considered to have Nazi sympathies and antecedents' won power, even if only in partnership.

Thousands of people began demonstrating every day against the coalition in the towns and cities of Austria. Austria's 14 partners in the European Union imposed sanctions to register their disapproval in the strongest terms. On February 28, Haider resigned as leader of the Party in Vienna, while retaining his governorship. It was a characteristically fascist tactical retreat.

CREATING A POLITICAL PLATFORM

In India, the fascist Rashtriya Swayamsevak Sangh (RSS) is now at the centre of Indian politics. As it happens, the year 2000 marks an important milestone in the RSS's chequered career as well. It acquired a new Sarsanghchalak (supremo) on March 10, Kuppahali Seetaramaiyah Sudarshan, and its political wing the Bharatiya Janata Party did likewise on August 27. It was Bangaru Laxman, a Dalit and a south Indian. The contrasts were as obvious as the calculations underlying the ambiguity. Sudarshan is a hardliner; an unreconstructed Sanghi of old. He told Karan Thapar on BBC's *Hard Talk India* on August 14: 'We do not accept the concept of minorities at all.' The minorities must accept the 'culture' of the majority community. 'The Constitution does not reflect the ethos of the people' and 'we should evolve our own Constitution.'

Bangaru Laxman made a pitch for Muslim support at the BJP National Council's meeting on August 27 for reasons which are not hard to understand. The BJP chafes at the constraints imposed by the politics of coalition. It dominates the NDA but would prefer to be free to implement its own agenda. It, however, realizes that it has reached a plateau and is frustrated that the take-off stage is nowhere in sight. The BJP is forced to reckon with the strengths of Indian secularism, with India's plural society and the diversities of its national life. In Uttar Pradesh its strength in the Lok Sabha dwindled from 57 seats in 1998 to 30 only a year and a half later. Its prospects in the Assembly elections due in 2001 are bleak. In 1998 the BJP and its allies in the NDA had 265 seats based on 42.2 per cent of the popular vote. In 1999, the NDA could get no more than 296 seats based on 40.8 per cent of the popular vote.[1] In March 2000, the BJP failed to dislodge Laloo Prasad Yadav's Rashtriya Janata Dal from power. The Governor V.C. Pande swore in the BJP's ally, Samata Party's Nitish Kumar as Chief Minister only to be snubbed by the Assembly. Rabri Devi returned to office as Chief Minister.

While the Ayodhya plank holds no promise, it cannot be abandoned either. Yet, if revived, it is certain to repel many in the floating vote. Hence, the attempt to woo the Muslims, but not the Muslims alone. Bangaru Laxman was wooing even more ardently secular-minded Hindus who find the BJP's politics revolting. Significantly, he offered no assurances to Christians whom the RSS and its fronts, the VHP and the Bajrang Dal, have been systematically targeting for attacks ever since the BJP assumed power in New Delhi in March 1998. Nor had he any assurance to offer to the Muslims on the VHP's frantic efforts to build a temple on the site of the demolished mosque at Ayodhya. The VHP's 250-member central body, Kendriya Marga-darshak Mandal, comprising sadhus representing various sects, will meet at Allahabad in January 2001 to announce an 'auspicious' date for the construction of the temple. In July 2000 the VHP met at Agra and informed the nation that it is 'ready to build the temple in Ayodhya by March 2001.' (*TT* August 27, 2000). The VHP General Secretary Praveen Togadia confirmed in a statement on August 27 that construction of the temple would begin after March 2001. He revealed that 80 of the 108 pillars were ready for use.

The BJP's record notwithstanding, Bangaru Laxman told its National Council, on August 27: 'There is nothing in our ideology, policies and programme for any one to surmise that we should not, or cannot, reach out to the Muslims.' The BJP could improve over its 1998 election performance only marginally, he admitted, because the Muslims did not vote for it. 'We have somehow taken it for granted that our party will not receive any significant support from them [the Muslims].' But he had nothing concrete to offer them. He could hardly do any better without alienating the RSS.

Bangaru Laxman himself had admitted on the previous day, August 26, that the basic ideology of the BJP and the RSS was the same (*IE* August 27). The differences could be sorted out. The BJP felt that its 'distinguishing features' – the three issues 'frozen' in order to drum up the NDA coalition, Ram temple at Ayodhya, a uniform civil code, and abrogation of Article 370 of the Constitution – 'were not necessary *now*'. These words are strikingly reminiscent of those used by Atal Behari Vajpayee in the same context two years ago. Asked by Dina Vakil 'to elaborate on that oft-repeated phrase "not on our agenda" apropos the mosques at Kashi and Mathura, Vajpayee replied "It means they are not on our agenda *for the time being*. Nobody can say what will happen in future. But as I have said in my interview they are not on our agenda. Full stop."' (*TOI* January 8, 1998). Given his belief that construction of a Ram temple at Ayodhya was necessary 'to save honour of the Hindu community' (*TOI* May 13, 1991) it was remarkable that he chose to include it among the 'frozen' issues in order to acquire power.

This explains why the RSS has been so understanding. It suits the BJP to 'freeze' the three issues in order to form a government. As Vajpayee admitted in Mumbai on December 26, 1997, the BJP was 'in the power game.' This is precisely what the RSS expected of the BJP. Its chief Rajendra Singh said during the 1998 election campaign, 'There is nothing wrong if a political party formulates new strategies to come to power . . . the pace of seva [sic] activities of the RSS and other activities was slow. *A Central Government with a positive outlook would remove many hurdles in our way. This would benefit the country in general and the Hindu society in particular*' (*Organiser*, February 22, 1998). Rajendra Singh's successor, K.S. Sudarshan, had the same expectations (*TS* March 17, 2000). Yubaraj Ghimire reported (*IE* March 27, 1998) how the RSS planned to make the most of the 'pro-Hindutva atmosphere'. Bangaru Laxman dispelled all doubts in the minds of the RSS by assuring it in an interview, significantly to its organ *Panchjanya*, while the Nagpur session was on: 'Look here, the question of giving up Hindutva simply does not arise. After all, Hindutva is in-built in the party. When have I ever said the party is ready to give up its fundamental principles and ideology? Even today the BJP is wedded to these.' He acknowledged that 'among the issues that dominated, the Ramjanmabhoomi agitation played a major role.' This was in reply to a pointed question on what he reckoned to be the milestones in the BJP's progress (*TT* August 31, 2000).

Now, as before, the BJP faces the same dilemma which Walter K. Andersen and Shridhar D. Damle mentioned in their book: 'It is questionable if the BJP could survive politically without the RSS cadre, and the cadre will not stay unless the leadership of the party stays firmly in the hands of the "brotherhood".'[2] No wonder that while in Nagpur for the National Council meeting Vajpayee visited the RSS headquarters on August 27. (The top brass, however, were absent). He declared, 'The post [of Prime Minister] may go tomorrow, but I will always remain a humble swayamsevak.' He had joined the RSS *shakha* in Gwalior in 1939. On August 11, 2000 Vajpayee and Advani offered a month's salary as *guru dakshina* at a function held at Murli Manohar Joshi's residence in New Delhi. Doubtless, all three, and other senior BJP leaders besides, had taken the RSS pledge which reads thus:

Remembering Almighty God and my forebears, I take this oath. For the betterment of my sacred Hindu religion, Hindu culture, and Hindu community, I will devote myself to the prosperity of my Holy Motherland. I swear that I shall serve the Rashtriya Swayamsevak Sangh with my body, my mind, and my money. I will be faithful to this oath throughout my life.

In yet another of the contradictions with which the Sangh *parivar* (family) bristles, the Nagpur National Council was administered a firm warning about the limits of dissent even as its President tried to project a liberal image.

Vajpayee and Finance Minister Yashwant Sinha were sent the party's resolutions 'for their approval before being finalized' as General Secretary M. Venkaiah Naidu revealed (*TH* August 22). Vajpayee told the Council on August 27 that 'politics should be practised only to a limit. We have to draw a Lakshman rekha and should not go beyond that.' He added: 'In matters of governance, the decision of the Prime Minister has to be final' (*IE* August 28). The next day it was Advani's turn to scold members: 'They have to get over their old habit of publicly pointing out Government's shortcomings when they were in opposition . . . the family's shortcomings should not be discussed publicly.' Dissent was thus stifled in the only forum where it can and should be expressed – the General Body. The BJP is as fascist as its parent, the RSS.

The Italian scholar Marzia Casolari has revealed, on the basis of archival evidence, the RSS's links with and admiration for Mussolini's fascist regime.[3] If there has been no sharp international reaction to the assumption of power in New Delhi by the RSS, through its political arm the Bharatiya Janata Party (BJP), as there was in Austria, it is because the RSS and the BJP have skillfully wormed their way into the mainstream of Indian politics since the 1970s. In 2000, another RSS front, the Vishwa Hindu Parishad, which has been in the forefront of the movement to demolish the Babri Masjid in Ayodhya, is knocking frantically on the doors of the United Nations Economic and Social Council demanding a 'consultative status' with the Council (*CC* July 2000).

The RSS has, indeed, come a long way since it was founded at Nagpur in September 1925 on the festival of Dussehra which commemorates the victory of Shri Ram over the demon King Ravana.[4] Its founder was Keshav Baliram Hedgewar, a medical doctor. His mentor, Balkrishna Shivram Moonje, sent him to Calcutta in 1910 to pursue his medical studies and – unofficially – to learn terrorist techniques from the Bengal secret societies. On returning to Nagpur in 1915, he followed Moonje into the Congress. Both became disenchanted with it before long. Andersen and Damle record how

> during this period of escalating Hindu–Muslim animosity in Nagpur, Hedgewar began to develop the intellectual foundations of the RSS. A major influence on his thinking was a handwritten manuscript of Vinayak Damodar Savarkar's *Hindutva*, which advanced the thesis that the Hindus were a nation. The central propositions of Savarkar's manuscript are that Hindus are the indigenous people of the sub-continent and that they form a single national group.[5]

V.D. Savarkar's older brother G.D. (Babarao) Savarkar helped the RSS to expand into Western Maharashtra.

Hedgewar died on June 21, 1940 and was succeeded by Madhav Sadashiv Golwalkar as Sarsanghchalak. The RSS grew under his leadership, but remained on the periphery of Indian politics as a militant Hindu group with a growing reputation for complicity in communal riots.

An understanding between Golwalkar and the Hindu Maha-sabha leader S.P. Mookerjee led to the floating of what became the political arm of the RSS, the Bharatiya Jana Sangh, on October 21, 1951. It merged into the Janata Party in March 1977 along with the Congress (O), Socialists, Bharatiya Lok Dal, and Congress for Democracy and shared power with them at the center. The government fell in July 1979. The Jan Sangh faction left the Janata Party and reinvented itself as the Bharatiya Janata Party (BJP) on April 5, 1980. The name was chosen calculatedly to distance itself from the past. It, however, lost little time in acknowledging its ancestry.

The BJP fared disastrously in the 1984 general election when it won a mere 2 seats and 7.4 per cent of the popular vote. Rajiv Gandhi's decision to open the locks at the gates of the Babri Masjid in February 1986 gave the BJP a shot in the arm. On June 11, 1989, at Palampur, its National Executive adopted a resolution on Ayodhya with an eye to the general elections due in November. It demanded that 'the sentiments of the overwhelming majority in this country – the Hindus' be respected and 'the site in dispute should be handed over to the Hindus and a mosque built at some other place.' Though left unsaid, the demand was clear – the Babri mosque which stood on the site should be demolished. And demolished it was three years later, on December 6, 1992. To charge the atmosphere suitably, the BJP's President L.K. Advani waded through pools of blood in his *rath yatra* (mammoth religious procession) in 1990 from Somnath temple in Gujarat to Ayodhya. If in 1989 the BJP won 85 seats and 11.4 per cent of the votes, in 1991 it secured 120 seats and 20.1 per cent of the votes.

To no small extent the BJP owes the rise in its fortunes also to disunity among the secular parties and to the virtual complicity of P.V. Narasimha Rao's government (1991–96) in the demolition of the Babri Masjid. The BJP prospered – it won 161 seats and 21.34 per cent of the votes in 1996; and these figures went up to 180 and 25.6 respectively in 1998, when it found a coalition government of the National Democratic Alliance. For 1999 the figures are 182 seats and 23.7 per cent of the votes. Never for a moment did 'the architect of this victory', L.K. Advani, who was constrained to yield the crown at the last moment in 1995 to Atal Behari Vajpayee, conceal the cynical calculations that governed his actions.

Immediately on the passing of the Palampur resolution on Ayodhya on June 11, 1989, Advani said, 'I am sure it will translate into votes.' On December 3, 1989, after the general elections, he expressed satisfaction that the issue had contributed to the BJP's success. On February 24, 1991, as India teetered towards another election, he was confident that the issue would 'influence the electoral verdict in favour of the BJP.' On June 18, 1991 he made this pathetic confession: 'Had I not played the Ram factor effectively, I would have definitely lost from the New Delhi constituency.' Shortly after the demolition of the Babri Mosque on December 6, 1992, and another wave of carnage that came in its train, Advani wrote that if the Muslims were to identify themselves with the concept of Hindutva there would not be any reason for riots to take place (*TOI* January 30, 1993). In July 1992, he argued in the Lok Sabha Speaker's chamber: 'You must recognize the fact that from two seats in Parliament in 1985 we have come to 117 seats in 1991. This has happened primarily because we took up this issue [Ayodhya].' Behind the BJP's religio-cultural rhetoric, however, there has always been cold political calculation. BJP leader Sushma Swaraj ripped apart this pretence in Bhopal on April 14, 2000, when she admitted that the Ram Janmabhoomi movement was 'purely political in nature and had nothing to do with religion' (*TT* April 16, 2000).

DECEPTION AND DECEIT

This habit of dressing up political objectives in a quasi-religious rhetoric goes back to the origins of Hindutva itself. In 1923, the Hindu Mahasabha leader, V.D. Savarkar, wrote a pamphlet propounding the two-nation theory. It was entitled *Hindutva: Who is a Hindu?* and was published under the *nom de plume* 'A Maratha', since he was in prison. A second and authoritative edition appeared in 1942. Its publisher, S.S. Savarkar, wrote in the Preface:

> Apart from the religious aspect involved in the conception of the words 'Hindu' and 'Hinduism', Veer Savarkar had to *coin some new words* such as *'Hindutva'*, 'Hinduness', 'Hindudom' in order to express totality of the cultural, historical, and above all the national aspects along with the religious one, which mark out the Hindu People as a whole. *The definition is not consequently meant to be a definition of Hindu Dharma, or Hindu religion.* It is a definition of 'Hindutva', 'Hinduness'.

V.D. Savarkar himself wrote in his book *Hindutva* that '*Hindutva is not identical with what is vaguely indicated by the term Hinduism.*'

Jawaharlal Nehru, the most articulate exponent of India's ideal of secularism, foresaw the peril. 'The danger to India, mark you, is not communism. It is Hindu right-wing communalism' he told officers of India's Foreign Service.[6]

One of Nehru's greatest services to India was his perceptive, almost prophetic, insight into the insidious nature of Hindu communalism. It had infected his own party, the Congress. On September 6, 1951, he complained publicly of Congressmen talking in a communal voice. Not that he was blind to Muslim communalism. But, as he told the All India Congress Committee (AICC) on May 11, 1958, the 'communalism of the majority is far more dangerous than the communalism of the minority.' On January 5, 1961, he noted that 'communalism is a part of our society' and explained why Hindu communalism was far more dangerous. 'When the minority communities are communal, you can see that and understand it. But *the communalism of a majority community is apt to be taken for nationalism.*'

Justice P. Venugopal, who sat on the Commission which inquired into the communal flare-up in Kanyakumari district in March 1982, indicted the RSS severely:

The RSS adopts a militant and aggressive attitude and sets itself as the champion of what it considers to be the rights of Hindus against minorities. It has taken upon itself the task to teach the minority their place and if they are not willing to learn their place, teach them a lesson. The RSS has given respectability to communalism and communal riots and demoralize administration [sic]. The RSS methodology for provoking communal violence is:

a) rousing communal feelings in the majority community by the propaganda that Christians are not loyal citizens of this country;

b) deepening the fear in the majority community by a clever propaganda that the population of the minorities is increasing and that of Hindus decreasing;

c) infiltrating into the administration and inducing the members of the civil and police services by adopting and developing communal attitudes;

d) training young people of the majority community in the use of weapons like dagger, sword and spear;

e) spreading rumours to widen the communal cleavage and deepen communal feelings by giving colour to any trivial incident.

The RSS shakhas include in their programmes training in lathis, swords, javelin throw. Drills, exercises, parades and other activities are organized in playgrounds and other public places. All these activities are organized in the name of physical training. The aim behind these activities appears to be to inculcate an attitude of militancy and *training for any kind of civil strife*. They often cause apprehension, fear and a sense of insecurity among the minorities. It prejudicially affects maintenance of public tranquility.

The RSS's more recent vandalism on the sets of Deepa Mehta's projected film *Water* in January–February 2000 is of a piece with its record on freedom of speech and expression. In March 1991, Ashok Singhal, general secretary of the RSS front Vishwa Hindu Parishad, denounced the film based on the novel *Shaher Mein Curfew* (*City Under Curfew*) by Vibhuti Rai: 'Cinema halls screening this film will be burnt down.' Anand Patwardhan's award-winning film on Ayodhya, *Ram Ke Nam* (*In the Name of Ram*) could not be screened in December 1992 because men of the RSS student front Akhil

Bharatiya Vidyarthi Parishad (ABVP) stormed Hinduja College in Bombay (*TOI* December 27, 1992).

Deceit and deception are integral to the RSS–BJP strategy. The BJP's earlier incarnation, the Jan Sangh, put up a false case before the Commission of Inquiry which probed into the death of the Jan Sangh's President, Deen Dayal Upadhyaya, in February 1968. Justice Y.V. Chandrachud disbelieved the evidence of the Sangh's treasurer, Nana Deshmukh, on a vital point and found that a document it had produced before it was fabricated.

In November 1990, BJP General Secretary Krishan Lal Sharma claimed to have *seen* a copy of a Hindi weekly *Harijan Sewak* of July 27, 1937 allegedly containing Gandhi's views on the Ramjanmabhoomi (birth place at Ayodhya). He wrote a letter to Prime Minister Chandrashekhar quoting two paragraphs from the weekly. *The Times of India's* Research Bureau nailed the lie. Sharma also cited Volume 26, page 65 of *The Collected Works of Mahatma Gandhi* in support of his case. This was also exposed as a lie.[7]

A word about the forging of the RSS's political arm, the Jan Sangh. After Gandhi's assassination on January 30, 1948, the Constituent Assembly passed a resolution on April 3 which urged a ban on any political organization which 'excludes from its membership persons on grounds of religion, race and caste. . . .' Dr Shyama Prasad Mookerjee, a Hindu Mahasabha leader and member of Nehru's first Cabinet (1947–50), was party to this resolution. When he resigned from the Cabinet in April 1950, he realized that return to the Mahasabha would entail certain loss of credibility. The quest that he then began led him to a deal with the RSS supremo M.S. Golwalkar. His associate Balraj Madhok writes in his biography of Mookerjee:

> It was clear to [Mookerjee] . . . that he must have a political platform outside the Parliament to project his point of view. . . . [He] suggested to Hindu Mahasabha leaders that they should open their doors to all Indians, irrespective of their caste and creed and become a really democratic nationalist platform for men like him. This was not acceptable to Hindu Mahasabha. He therefore decided to create a new political platform. . . .
>
> [The RSS leaders had also] begun to feel the urgent need of a political organization *which could reflect the ideology and ideas of the RSS in the political sphere.* . . . The RSS approach to the problems of

culture, nationalism, and partition had his [Mookerjee's] fullest approval. He, therefore, instinctively felt that any political organization sponsored by, or enjoying the confidence of the RSS could surely and speedily become such a force in the political life of the country as may command his fullest allegiance and also succeed in mobilizing and consolidating the non-Congress and non-Communist nationalist public opinion into an effective opposition. . . .

It was decided that the RSS should continue to be a social and cultural organization as before but it should actively support a political party for the running of which it would spare some senior workers and allow its goodwill to be used by such a party. . . . A meeting was arranged between Dr Mookerjee and Shri Golwalkar. Dr Mookerjee with his eye on the forthcoming elections was in a hurry to form the new party of his conception. . . . It was in this meeting that the proposed party was tentatively christened 'Bharatiya Jan Sangh'—Indian People's Party. In the discussions of the day the approach of the proposed political party to the term 'Hindu Rashtra' and its political, social and cultural implications figured prominently. ,

Some of the persons present argued that though *they were in full agreement with the concept of 'Hindu Rashtra', yet they would not like it to be incorporated or used in the objectives of the proposed party because that might create misunderstanding in the minds of some people.* That provoked Dr Mookerjee who gave a convincing exposition of the concept of 'Hindu Rashtra' as he understood it. . . . But he was opposed to the word being imposed on those who were not, for the time being, prepared to accept it. He, therefore, suggested that the word Bharatiya and Indian, *which are synonyms of the word Hindu, but are more acceptable to those under the influence of West* as also to those who lack courage of conviction, should also be used along with the word Hindu till such people shed their inferiority complex and learn to take pride in their own name and traditions.[8]

This is surely a strange experiment in duplicity: the RSS, which professes to be a *'cultural* body', controls a *political party*. One dis-closure after another reveals the RSS in yet darker hues. If in 1994, Gopal Godse, brother of Gandhi's assassin revealed that earlier disclaimers were false and that they all belonged to the RSS, in 1998 were published the memoirs of Rajeshwar Dayal.[9] As Chief Secretary to the Government of Uttar Pradesh at the time of partition, he came across damning evidence of the RSS chief Golwalkar's plans to stage a pogram of Muslims. Yet Chief Minister Gobind Ballabh Pant refused to order his arrest. Golwalkar absconded and was arrested only after Gandhi's assassination.

It is of this organization that Prime Minister Atal Behari Vajpayee said on February 5, 2000: 'Rashtriya Swayamsevak Sangh is not a political outfit. It is a cultural and social organization and I do not think objections should be raised on anybody joining it.' This was in defence of the Gujarat government's order permitting civil servants to become members of the RSS. The President objected to this amendment. Predictably, Union Home Minister L.K. Advani, not only defended the move, but proceeded to declare that the Central Government would review the ban on its employees from participating in RSS activities.

It was left to the former Chief Minister of Uttar Pradesh Kalyan Singh to spill the beans. He said at Aligarh on February 8: 'I have spent a greater part of my life in this organization [RSS] and I can say that right from the distribution of election tickets [to candidates] in BJP to selecting Cabinet Ministers, it is only the RSS which calls the shots. What else is political activity?'

That the RSS, indeed, calls the shots was demonstrated by what followed. On February 11, the RSS supremo Rajendra Singh demanded that the bar be removed. Thereupon Vajpayee took up the matter with the RSS, after which Singh declared that 'The RSS will not mount any pressure on the centre' (*TH* February 14, 2000). On February 14 a relieved Vajpayee said, 'There will be no change in the existing law'. He owed the relief to the grace of the RSS boss.

This fragile balance can be upset any time by unforeseen developments. When it is upset, assuredly it is the will of the RSS that will prevail. The BJP will comply obediently.

2

THE RSS:
OUTLOOK AND POLICIES

Thanks to the respectability which the Jan Sangh gained during Jayaprakash Narayan's movement and in the Janata Party government, its mentor, the Rashtriya Swayamsevak Sangh, gained considerably. Between 1977 and 1982 the RSS growth was 'phenomenal', its then General Secretary Rajendra Singh proudly claimed on August 3, 1983. The total number of *shakhas* (branches) had increased from 6,000 to 19,000 and was expected to reach 21,000 by the end of 1983. If the smaller ones were included, the total would reach 35,000 with 700,000 dedicated swayamsevaks (volunteers) attending the daily drills and meetings at dawn or dusk. Today, in 2000, the RSS has 45,000 *shakhas* all over the country and a formidable organizational network. Bharat Bhushan describes it in detail:

> The only organization which has consistently geared itself to micro-level politics, getting into almost every sphere of activity which influences social and political life is the RSS. In the field of education, its front organization Vidya Bharati today is the largest educational organization in the non-governmental sector with 13,000 educational institutes including Saraswati Vidya Mandirs, 75,000 teachers and over 17 lakh students. It has organizations, headed by RSS volunteers, addressing tribals (Vanvasi Kalyan Ashram), literature (Akhil Bharatiya Sahitya Parishad),

intellectuals (Pragya Bharati, Deendayal Research Institute), historians (Bharatiya Itihas Sankalan Yojana), teachers (Bharatiya Shikshan Mandal and Akhil Bharatiya Rashtriya Shaikshik Mahasangh), language (Sanskrit Bharati), culture (Sanskar Bharati), slum-dwellers (Seva Bharati, Hindu Seva Pratishthan, Swami Vivekanand Medical Mission, National Medicos Organization), leprosy patients (Bharatiya Kushta Nivarak Sangh), cooperatives (Sahkar Bharati), consumers (Akhil Bharatiya Grahak Panchayat), publication of newspapers and other propaganda material (Bharat Prakashan, Suruchi Prakashan, Lokhit Prakashan, Gyanganga Prakashan, Archana Prakashan, Bharatiya Vichar Sadhana, Madhav Prakashan, Rashtrotthan Sahitya, Sadhana Pustak Prakashan and Akashvani Prakashan), scientists (Vigyan Bharati), caste integration (Samajik Samrasta Manch), religion and proselytization (Vivekananda Kendra, Vishwa Hindu Parishad, Hindu Jagaran Manch, Bajrang Dal), industrialists (Bharat Vikas Parishad), Sikhs (Rashtriya Sikh Sangat), ex-servicemen (Poorva-Sainik Seva Parishad), NRIs (Bharatiya Swayamsevak Sangh, Hindu Swayamsevak Sangh, Hindu Seva Sangh, Sanatana Dharma Swayamsevak Sangh, Friends of India Society International) – the list is virtually endless.

These organizations are in addition to its political front (BJP), trade union wing (Bharatiya Mazdoor Sangh), women's wing (Rashtriya Sevika Samiti), students wing (Akhil Bharatiya Vidyarthi Parishad), and its economic wing (Swadeshi Jagaran Manch). For the RSS, politics is not only about who can come into power and the quantum of patronage disbursed. That is why it does not see the battle for the hearts and minds of the people being fought only at the hustings but in almost all spheres of social activity. (*HT* March 3, 2000)

This is the many-headed monster that rules over the party leading the government at the centre and in many states.

CULTURE AND POLITICS

The RSS claims to be a 'cultural' body, devoted to 'national' uplift and committed to democracy and secularism. But the claim is challenged by all outside the Sangh *parivar* (family). The RSS is accused of bigoted communalism, addiction to violence and practice of deceit to capture political power. What, then, is the truth?

We can get a good idea of that straight from the horse's mouth in a solemn legal document. This is Miscellaneous Application No. 17

of 1978 filed in the court of the District Judge, Nagpur by Rajendra Singh and the then Sarsanghchalak Balasaheb Deoras's younger brother, Bhaurao, on behalf of the RSS. They were appealing against the decision of the Joint Charity Commissioner M.S. Vaidya, holding that the RSS was 'a public trust' and, therefore, liable to be registered under the Bombay Public Trusts Act, 1950.

Singh and Deoras recalled (in Para 8) that the RSS was founded on Dussehra Day 1925 by Dr K.B. Hedgewar for a particular reason: 'The concept that [sic] nation with a glorious past which, indeed, was a "Hindu Rashtra" was being wiped out from the people and *its interest was being ignored by the then political leaders* particularly after the eclipse of Lokmanya Tilak from the political horizon after his death in 1920.' The attack on Gandhi and the Congress was fairly clear.

'The concept of "Hindu nation" of the founder of RSS was on the basis of *cultural unity of the entire people living in the Bharat varsh*.' Lest any imagine that 'the entire people' were truly included, they emphasized that 'It is significant to note that the name was not chosen as "Hindu Swayamsevak Sangh" *though the Sangh is open to Hindus only*. This is because of the faith of the Sangh that in India "Rashtriya" (national) means "of Hindus" which are the mainstream of the Nation.' Another reason for the name was 'to reflect the *political ideology* of the organization, though the Sangh *as such* never had politics of its own *as of policy*.'

Failure to appreciate this fundamental stand of the RSS lies at the root of the continued misunderstanding of the RSS by some to this day. The RSS itself has, however, never wavered in its stand.

The Application states some important features of RSS ideology. Para 13 notes that 'The first feature is that the terms used have *special significance* and meaning as understood by the Organization in view of its philosophy as distinct from the *ordinary meaning*.' 'In brief . . . one has to look as to how [the said terms] *are understood by the organization and not how such terms are commonly used or interpreted by others*. Such terms are Rashtriya, Dharma (religion), Sanskriti (cultural), Hindu Dharma, etc.' This enables the RSS to practice duplicity freely.

Secondly, the Chief (Sarsanghchalak) is 'the guide and philosopher', and his writings and speeches are important. The 'written constitution came into existence for the first time in June 1949.' 'The third feature of the Constitution is its flexibility. . . . [The] fourth feature is that aims and objects are distinguished from policy . . . *policy is not a permanent feature* and changes or is changed from time to time.' The RSS does not participate in 'day to day politics though *the Sangh has a political philosophy* within its wide sweep of cultural work. *It is possible for Sangh to change this policy and even participate in politics.*'

There is the special importance of the flag, 'the "Bhagwa-Dhwaj," the age-old symbol of Hindu Culture.' Another feature is 'the limited democratic form and machinery provided for carrying out the work of the Sangh. . . . There is no election at all levels but selection and nomination except the posts Sakaryawaha (General Secretary) and Prant Sanghchalaks (State Chiefs).'

The document concludes: 'that the work of the RSS is neither religious nor charitable but its objects are cultural and patriotic as contra-distinguished from religious or charitable. *It is akin to political purposes* though RSS is not *at present* a political party inasmuch as the RSS Constitution quoted above bars active political participation by RSS, as such, as *a policy*. . . . Tomorrow *the policy could be changed and RSS could participate in even day to day political activity as a political party because policy is not a permanent or irrevocable thing.*' (Paras 18 and 19).

Individual members were, however, free to join any political party (Article 4). The document boldly asserted that the RSS was free to proclaim itself a political party some day. This stand has never been altered. It has been reaffirmed repeatedly; including by Deoras, the supremo, on November 15 and 16, 1987.

The character of this 'cultural body' is fully explained by the definition which the Sangh assigns to culture.

> [It] does not mean the popular or governmental limited meaning as pertaining to art, drama, music, dance, etc. The word 'Sanskritik' or cultural used in the Sangh work has a very wide sweep and has to be understood as expounded by the Guide and Philosopher of the RSS Shri Golwalkar in his speeches and writings. These include all aspects of society or nation; viz. *political*, social, economic, customary, morality, language, script and in general the Hindu way of life, inclusive of faiths of various groups in distinct tenets, practices, etc.

Contrast this assertion in Para 26 of the document with that in

Article 4 (b) of the Constitution – 'The Sangh as such, has no politics and is devoted *purely* to cultural work'. But, if 'cultural' means what the RSS application solemnly said it does, is not Article 4 (b) of its Constitution calculated to deceive? Curiously, the Application mentioned that the Income Tax Commissioner had held that the RSS was neither a religious nor a charitable body and therefore, not exempt from tax. But it deliberately omitted to mention what the RSS had contended in the tax proceedings.

In an appeal filed before the Appellate Assistant Commissioner of Income Tax, Nagpur (May 29, 1972), Balasaheb Deoras solemnly stated *the direct opposite*; namely, that it held the funds *on trust for charitable purposes* (Grounds 35, 36 and 37):

> The learned ITO erred in holding that the objects of the Sangh are not charitable . . . erred in holding that the funds were not proved to have been utilized for 'charitable purpose' . . . has not properly appreciated the connotation of the words 'Trust' and any other legal obligation' . . . failed to see that the assesses was under a legal obligation to spend the money for the objects specified in the Constitution . . . .

These contradictions apart, the RSS behaved shabbily in the proceedings. On October 15, 1973, it conceded before K.H. Chainani, the ITO, that 'all policy decisions were communicated' to the 18 Prant Officers. Only a fortnight later, it 'resiled from this position', Chainani noted with disgust. On October 21, 1973, an amended Constitution was filed before him. But, the amendments were not shown to the Joint Charity Commissioner who complained of this in his Order of January 11, 1978.

The amendments were made only for tax purposes. Article 5 was amended to make the flag an object of worship 'which the Sangh regards as its Guru'. This was to save the huge Gurudakshina offerings from tax. Article 22 was amended to make the Gurudakshina received by each branch 'the funds of that Shakha', not of the central organization.

If the Sangh can resort to such stratagem for filthy lucre, what will it not do to grab power? The thought is not absent from its leaders' minds. On September 16, 1979 UNI reported that Deoras 'said . . . that his organization would in ten years gain the popularity needed to form a Government at the Centre. "Nobody can grudge such an eventuality in a democratic set up," he told a closed-door meeting attended by nearly 100 people [in Bhopal].' Three days later, Deoras rushed back to Bhopal to contradict the report. The RSS mouthpiece *Organiser* angrily denied the report and quoted Deoras as saying that it was not a closed door meeting at all and the entire proceedings had been taped and played back 'a few days back to local correspondents and they were all satisfied . . .'. UNI, however, carried another story on September 20 which said that Deoras 'refused to oblige newsmen who insisted on listening to the taped version' despite the RSS local unit's promise to play the tapes at his press conference.

THE RSS BIBLE

The scholar Jean A. Curran characterized Madhav Sadashiv Golwalkar's book *We or our Nationhood Defined* as the RSS's 'Bible' in his sympathetic book *Militant Hinduism in Indian Politics: A Study of the RSS* (1951). Golwalkar's 77-page book was written in 1938 when he was appointed RSS General Secretary by Hedgewar (whom he succeeded as Sarsanghchalak in 1940). So brutally candid is *We or Our Nationhood Defined* that a desperate attempt was made by the RSS to distance itself from it – the RSS claimed that the book was merely an English translation of the Marathi work *Rashtra Meemansa* by Babarao G.D. Savarkar, brother of V.D. Savarkar. However, in his Preface to *We or Our Nationhood Defined* dated March 22, 1939, Golwalkar described *Rashtra Meemansa* as 'one of my chief sources of inspiration and help. An English translation of this is due to be shortly out [*sic*].'[1]

Rajendra Singh and Bhaurao Deoras made an authoritative statement on that book in Para 10 of their 1978 application: 'With a view to give a scientific base to propagate the idea India being [*sic*] historically from time immemorial a Hindu Nation, late Shri M.S. Golwalkar had written a book entitled, "We or Our Nationhood Defined".' In Para 7 they 'placed on record' his book *Bunch of Thoughts* (1966) in order 'to clarify and understand the true purpose, the exact nature, the ambit and scope of the RSS work . . . and its activities.' The RSS appeal thus affirmed the continuing validity and relevance of Golwalkar's writings, specifically of those two books.

Sample these extracts from *We*:

'Ever since that evil day, when Moslems first landed in Hindusthan, right up to the present moment, the Hindu Nation has been gallantly fighting on to shake off the despoilers. . . . The Race Spirit has been awakening.'

Referring to the secular nationalism of Gandhi and others, Golwalkar asserted that 'Effort was made to put the race on the wrong track' by propagating the concept of *territorial* nationalism. He went on to say:

> The idea was spread that for the first time the people were going to live a National life, the Nation in the land naturally was composed of all those who happened to reside therein and that all these people were to unite on a common 'National' platform and win back 'freedom' by 'Constitutional means'. Wrong notions of democracy strengthened the view and we began to class ourselves with our old invaders and foes under the outlandish name – Indian – and tried to win them over to join hands with us in our struggle. The result of this poison is too well known. We have allowed ourselves to be duped into believing our foes to be our friends and with our hands are undermining true Nationality.

This 'scientific' study lists five factors which make a Nation – geography, race, religion, culture, and language – and mentions the Jews as an instance of a Nation deprived of its land by the Romans and later by 'the engines of destruction loose under the name of Islam.' In other places,

> where religion does not form a distinguishing factor, culture together with the other necessary constituents of the Nation idea become the important point in the making up of individual Nationality. On the other hand in Hindusthan, Religion is an all-absorbing entity. Based as it is on the unshakable foundations of a sound philosophy of life (as indeed Religion ought to be), it has become eternally woven into the life of the Race, and forms, as it were, its very Soul. *With us, every action in life, individual, social or political, is a command of Religion.* We make war or peace, engage in arts and crafts, amass wealth and give it away, indeed we are born and we die – all in accord with religious injunctions. Naturally, therefore, we are what our great Religion has made us. Our Race-spirit is a child of our Religion and so with us *Culture is but a product of our all-comprehensive Religion*, a part of its body and not distinguishable from it.

Politics is to be conducted 'as one of the commands of Religion.'

Every Nation 'does profess and maintain a National Religion and culture, these being necessary to complete the Nation idea.'

What of the non-Hindus?

> All those not belonging to the national, i.e. Hindu race, Religion, Culture and Language, naturally fall out of the pale of real 'National' life.
>
> We repeat: in Hindusthan, the land of the Hindus, lives and should live the Hindu Nation – satisfying all the five essential requirements of the scientific nation concept of the modern world. Consequently only those movements are truly 'National' as aim at re-building, revitalizing and emancipating from its present stupor, the Hindu Nation. Those only are nationalist patriots, who, with the aspiration to glorify the Hindu race and Nation next to their heart, are prompted into activity and strive to achieve that goal. *All others are either traitors and enemies to the National cause, or, to take a charitable view, idiots.*

The 'idiots' can be cured, though:

> The foreign races in Hindusthan must either adopt the Hindu culture and language, must learn to respect and hold in reverence Hindu religion, must entertain no idea but those of the glorification of the Hindu race and culture, i.e., of the Hindu nation and must loose their separate existence to merge in the Hindu race, or may stay in the country, wholly subordinated to the Hindu Nation, claiming nothing, deserving no privileges, far less any preferential treatment – *not even citizen's rights*. There is, at least, should be, no other course for them to adopt. We are an old nation; let us deal, as old nations ought to and do deal, with the foreign races, who have chosen to live in our country.

Golwalkar left none in doubt as to the techniques of cure he favoured:

> To keep up the purity of the Race and its culture, Germany shocked the world by her [*sic*] purging the country of the Semitic Races – the Jews. Race pride at its highest has been manifested here. Germany has also shown how well nigh impossible it is for Races and cultures, having differences going to the root, to be assimilated into one united whole, a good lesson for us in Hindusthan to learn and profit by.

Educated Hindus are sneered at:

> This 'educated' class of Hindus became in truth slaves of the English,

as the late Dr S.V. Ketkar has aptly described them. They had cut their traces, lost their footing in the National past, and become deculturized, denationalized people. But they also formed the bulk of the 'Congress' and found no difficulty in eagerly gulping down the extra-ordinary absurdity, that their country was not theirs, but belonged to strangers and enemies of their Race equally with them.

Is this 'communalism'? Of course not. Golwalkar cries in hurt: 'How can we be "communal" having, as we do, no other interests but those relating on our country, our Nation?'

When one turns to his book *Bunch of Thoughts*, published a quarter century later, one is amazed at the continuity of the refrain. If anything, it is more strident. 'It is the grand world-unifying thought of Hindus alone that can supply the abiding basis for human brotherhood'. Their history 'stands in glowing contrast to the bloodstained pages of the history of expansion of Islam, Christianity and now Communism. . . .'

He condemned democracy and communism with equal fervour. Democracy? 'The high-sounding concept of "individual freedom" only meant the freedom of those talented few to exploit the rest . . .'. Democracy 'is to a very large extent only a myth in practice.'

He approvingly recalled 'our forefathers' who said 'the Hindu People, is our God'. Why, 'a comparative study – even by the foreign historians and travellers of those days – tells us that *the average man of this country was at one time incomparably superior to the average man of the other lands* . . . long before the West had learnt to eat roast meat instead of raw, we were one nation, with one motherland.'

Difference from others begins at the very birth of a Hindu.

Some wise men of today tell us that no man is born as Hindu or Muslim or Christian but as a simple human being. This may be true about others. But for a Hindu, he gets the first samskar when he is still in the mother's womb, and the last when his body is consigned to the flames. There are sixteen samaskars for the Hindu which make him what he is. In fact, we are Hindus even before we emerge from the womb of our mother. We are therefore born as Hindus. About the others, they are born to this world as simple unnamed human beings and later on, either circumcised or baptized, they become Muslims or Christians.

The RSS seeks to reclaim people who are born inferior at birth.

'Everybody knows that only a handful of Muslims came here as enemies and invaders. So, also, only a few foreign Christian missionaries came here. Now the Muslims and Christians have enormously grown in number.' This was either by force or deception. So, 'it is our duty to call these our forlorn brothers, suffering under religious slavery for centuries, back to their ancestral home . . . come back and identify themselves with their ancestral Hindu way of life in dress, customs, performing marriage ceremonies and funeral rites and such other things.'

The concept of territorial nationalism is rejected:

> They forgot that here was already a full-fledged ancient nation of the Hindus and the various communities which were living in the country were here either as *guests*, the Jews and Parsis, or as *invaders*, the Muslims and Christians. They never faced the question how all such heterogeneous groups could be called as children of the soil merely because, by an accident, they happened to reside in a common territory under the rule of a common enemy.

The Congress was the villain of the piece, since it accepted territorial nationalism.

> Most of the tragedies and evils that have overtaken our country during the last few decades and are even today corroding our national life are its direct outcome . . . In their phantom chase of achieving new unity and new nationality, our leaders raised the slogan of 'Hindu-Muslim unity'. . . . The first thing they preached was that our nationality could not be called Hindu, that even our land could not be called by its traditional name Hindusthan, as that would have offended the Muslim. *The name 'India' given by the British was accepted.* Taking that name, the 'new nation' was called the 'Indian Nation'. And the Hindu was asked to rename himself as 'Indian'.

That Gandhi was singled out for attack is understandable. The ground for the attack reveals a lot.

> But here, we had leaders who were, as if, pledged to *sap all manliness from their own people.* However, this is not a mere accident of history. This leadership only came as a bitter climax of the despicable tribe of so many of our ancestors who *during the past twelve hundred years* sold their national honour and freedom to foreigners, and *joined hands with*

the inveterate enemies of our country [read Muslims] and our religion in cutting the throats of their own kith and kin to gratify their personal egoism, selfishness and rivalry. No wonder nemesis overtook such a people in the form of such *a self-destructive leadership.*

Not that others are spared. 'The framers of our present Constitution also were not firmly rooted in the conviction of our single homogenous nationhood [as] is evident from the federal structure of our Constitution.'

Golwalkar was amazed that his call to the Muslims and Christians to embrace Hinduism should have aroused a furore. In an interview (*Nawakal* January 1 and 2, 1969) he explained that it was an appeal 'to return to their home.' They might, he graciously conceded, offer prayers 'on re-entering the Hindu fold, in the way in which one was doing earlier.' But, 'no room should be left for disharmony.' In everything else, they must conform and look upon only *'persons of our country as our ideal.'*

There was nothing new about his appeal. In a speech in 1960 he had characterized Muslims, Christians, Jews and Parsis as 'guests, but they are not the children of the soil.' It was published in a pamphlet titled *Why Hindu Rashtra?* He amplified: 'Unfortunately in our country our Constitution has equated the children of the soil with the aggressor, and given equal rights to everybody, just as a person without understanding may give equal rights to his children and to the thieves in his house and distribute the property among all.'

'HINDU' OR 'RASHTRIYA'?

This is the ideological legacy which Deoras acquired when he became Sarsanghchalak in 1973. He stuck to the line doggedly and was able to ward off pressures from Jayaprakash Narayan and some in the Janata Party to discard the legacy in 1977–79 by skilful prevarications. In an interview published on January 14, 1974, Deoras drew 'a distinction between religions which have risen from the Indian soil like Hinduism, Sikhism and Buddhism on the one hand and those like Islam and Christianity which have come from outside.' On November 7, 1982 he defined 'Hindu' in identical terms and then said 'Indeed, Hindu is National'. In between, he had made much play about widening the meaning of the word Hindu. On December 19, 1979, he went so far as to assert that the definition of the word *had been widened* and a large number of people of various religions were RSS volunteers. How this could have been done without amending the RSS Constitution, which restricts membership to Hindu males, he did not explain. The RSS has always kept its membership records secret; this despite the promise it made when the ban was lifted after the Gandhi assassination.

But in classic RSS doublespeak, he would use the word in two different senses *in one and the same pronouncement.* 'All those who feel attuned to this life current of our national culture – *irrespective of their religious creeds* are Hindus', he said at Nagpur on September 30, 1979, only to qualify it thus: 'The guarantee for [India's] secular character is not to be found merely in our Constitution nor in the assurance of a couple of leaders. It lies in *the Hindu society which forms the overwhelming majority in this country.*'

Several instances of such double talk can be cited. For instance, on October 19, 1979, on the eve of the 1980 census, he appealed to all sections of Hindus to indicate their religion as 'Hindu' *and also their castes within brackets.* This would help in retaining the majority character of the Hindus which the RSS would fight for, he explained. Exactly a month earlier, he said that the word had been widened to include others as well. And again: 'We consider all the natives of this land as Hindus, irrespective of religion'; but the RSS's 'main stress is on organizing traditional Hindus' (*Organiser* April 6, 1980).

Deoras kept steadfastly to the Golwalkar line. On January 15, 1983 he proclaimed in a manner reminiscent of Golwalkar: 'We reject geographical nationalism.' 'Nationalism has its roots in people's minds, in their ways of thinking, their sentiments. That is why we stick to the word "Hindu" . . . Life here revolves round the Hindu Society.' The minorities need not feel insecure living in a strong Hindu India because Hindus are known for their tolerance.

On September 11, 1983 he remarked, 'Some people say we should replace the expression "Hindu Rashtra" by "Bharatiya Rashtra,"' a reference to the BJP President, Atal Behari Vajpayee's plea to that effect in a recent issue of *Panchjanya*, the RSS Hindi weekly. 'There is no objection to "Bharatiya." But if anybody wants to change it because he is ashamed of the word "Hindu" we cannot accept the suggestion. After all, the word "Hindu" is more current than the word "Bharatiya."'

It was a sneering retort but not a surprising one. For, Golwalkar had said in his *Bunch of Thoughts* that while Bharatiya 'connotes the same meaning' as Hindu, 'it is commonly used as a translation of the word "Indian" which includes all the various communities like the Muslim, Christian, Parsi, etc. residing in this land. So, the word "Bharatiya" too is likely to mislead us when we want to denote our particular society. The word "Hindu" alone connotes correctly and completely the meaning that we want to convey.' Further: *'In this land of ours, Bharat, the national life is of the Hindu People. In short, this is the Hindu Nation.'*

Golwalkar reveals that when the RSS was given its name some felt it should bear the prefix 'Hindu', not 'Rashtriya', lest its *'doors should have to be kept open to all other people in the country.'* Hedgewar ridiculed the idea. 'Doctorji used to say that in our land the word "Rashtriya" naturally means "Hindu" and, therefore, the word "Hindu" need not be used.'

Such an exclusive concept can be inspired by hate alone and can only generate yet greater hate. To say that Hinduism 'despite the degenerating contact with the debased civilizations of the Musalmans and the Europeans, for the last ten centuries, is still the noblest in the world' is, surely, to promote group hatred.

As for the Muslim, 'if we glorify woman as a symbol of sacred motherhood he [the Muslim] would like to molest her. He was tooth and nail opposed to our way of life in all aspects – religious, cultural, social, etc.' (*Bunch of Thoughts*). The Muslim can be reclaimed only if he reverts to 'the original dress, language, view of life etc.' The form of worship may be retained but 'Muslims should have no objection to bringing Islam in line with reason and so-facilitate their passage back to the mother society.' Deoras repeated the stereotype of the marauding Muslim, on April 4, 1980: 'History says that Muslim conversion was by force all over the world'; and again: 'Christians and Muslims have had wars of religion, has anybody ever heard of any religious wars among Hindus?' (September 11, 1983).

HOLDING AN EMPIRE WITHOUT BECOMING EMPEROR

Golwalkar had bared the RSS's ambitions and technique as far back as 1949: 'If the Congress completely disintegrates and anarchy rules the country and there is nobody to take over . . . we may sacrifice part of our normal cultural activities and accept the responsibility.' Asked point blank 'Is it a fact that the Sangh plans to capture power?', he replied: 'We have kept before ourselves the ideal of Bhagwan Shri Krishna who held a big empire under his thumb but refused to become an emperor himself.' Or, as Rajendra Singh and Bhaurao Deoras said in Para 38 of their Application, 'The RSS desires to *dominate* the world by cultural conquest by a great process of true national regeneration'. The ideal can be fully realized if the BJP, kept under the RSS thumb, captures power as the 'national alternative.'

Interestingly, the British had, after careful deliberation, made sound assessment of the RSS. A circular sent by the Home Department of the Government of India to the Bihar government (No. F 201/44 Ests. Dated March 16, 1944) said: 'After a protracted consideration of the question in which the Governments of the C.P. and Berar and Bombay were also consulted, as the organization was strongest there, it was decided that the RSS was a politico-commercial organization which concentrated on the formation of a militant body on fascist lines. . . .'

The word fascist was aptly chosen. As Donald E. Smith says in his classic *India as a Secular State* (1963): 'The leader principle, the stress on militarism, the doctrine of racial-cultural superiority, ultra-nationalism infused with religious idealism, the use of symbols of past greatness, the emphasis on national solidarity, the exclusion of religious or ethnic minorities from the nation-concept – all of these features of the RSS are highly reminiscent of fascist movements in Europe.'[2]

The 1978 Application proudly claimed, as we have noted, that one of the RSS's distinctive features is 'the limited democratic form and machinery.' This is a breach of the solemn assurance on the basis of which the ban on the RSS, imposed after Gandhi's assassination in 1948, was lifted by the Government of India in 1949. On July 17, 1949 Patel wrote to Nehru: 'It was only after I had made him agree to a satisfactory constitution for the RSS and got some assurances and undertakings in regard to the Sangh policy for the future that I thought it safe to release [Golwalkar].' What were those 'assurances and undertakings'? The Government communiqué of February 4, 1948 announcing the ban said:

The professed aims and objects of the Rashtriya Swayamsevak Sangh are to promote the physical, intellectual and moral well-being of the Hindus and also to foster feelings of brotherhood, love and service amongst them. . . . Government have, however, noticed with regret that in practice members of Rashtriya Swayamsevak Sangh have not adhered to their professed ideals. Undesirable and even dangerous activities have been carried on by the members of the Sangh. It has been found that in several parts of the country individual members of the Rashtriya Swayamsevak Sangh have indulged in acts of violence involving arson, robbery, dacoity and murder and have collected illicit arms and ammunitions. They have been found circulating leaflets, exhorting people to resort to terrorist methods, to collect firearms, to create disaffection against the Government and suborn the Police and Military.

On February 6, Golwalkar gave a directive to 'disband the RSS till the ban is there' while 'denying all the charges.' He claimed that the RSS was law-abiding and would 'carry on its activities within the bounds of law.' Golwalkar was released on August 6, 1948 but his movements were restricted to Nagpur. Five days later he wrote to Nehru and Patel complaining against the restrictions. On September 27, A.V. Pai replied from the Prime Minister's Secretariat that

Government have a great deal of evidence in their possession to show that the RSS were engaged in activities which were anti-national and prejudicial from the point of view of public good. . . . Even after the ban we have received information about the undesirable activities of the old members of the RSS. This information continues to come to us even now. You will appreciate that in view of this, the Government cannot consider the RSS as such a harmless organization from the public point of view.

Golwalkar demanded an enquiry on November 3. By now the restriction had been lifted for the sole purpose of permitting him to visit Delhi and lay his case before the government. However, his request for an interview with Nehru was refused. Nehru made a telling point:

It would appear that the declared objectives have little to do with the real ones and with the activities carried on in various forms and ways by people associated with the RSS. These real objectives appear to be completely opposed to the decisions of the Indian Parliament and provisions of the proposed Constitution, anti-national and often subversive and violent.

And Patel, who was otherwise not hostile to the RSS, had earlier written to his Hindu Mahasabha colleague in the cabinet, S.P. Mookerjee on July 18 that

> our reports do confirm that, as a result of the activities of these two bodies, particularly the former [the RSS], an atmosphere was created in the country in which such a ghastly tragedy [Gandhiji's assassination] became possible. There is no doubt in my mind that the extreme section of the Hindu Mahasabha was involved in this conspiracy. The activities of the RSS constituted a clear threat to the existence of Government and the State. Our reports show that those activities, despite the ban, have not died down. Indeed, as time has marched on, the RSS circles are becoming more defiant and are indulging in their subversive activities in an increasing measure.

Patel, however, did meet Golwalkar, but remained unconvinced that the ban should be lifted. Golwalkar was arrested on November 14, but he had issued a call the previous day to swayamsevaks to revive the organization and flout the ban. On December 9, he issued a call for satyagraha. This was withdrawn on January 14, 1949, after Patel and he had resumed contact through intermediaries. The principal demands that the government made in these negotiations were that the RSS constitution be reduced to writing and be made public, and that the RSS declare its allegiance to the Indian national flag. Golwalkar forwarded a written constitution to the government on April 11, 1949. The government was, however, not satisfied. On May 3, the Home Ministry replied through H.V.R. Iyengar who said the government wanted a 'specific declaration, under Article 4 [of Golwalkar's draft] of allegiance to the Constitution of India as established by law and an explicit acceptance, in Article 5, of the National Flag.' The government also insisted on 'the democratic elective principle' in the RSS. Golwalkar replied angrily on May 17 claiming that these demands were 'wholly out of place in the matter under consideration', and urging the government to 'recognize the difference between a constitution and an oath of allegiance.' This is highly significant and touches the core of the RSS credo.

However, discussions continued between the RSS and the government directly as well as through intermediaries, and finally the government issued a communiqué on July 11, 1949 announcing the lifting of the ban. The ban was being lifted, it was made clear, because

> the RSS leader has undertaken to make the loyalty to the Indian Constitution and respect for the National Flag more explicit in the constitution of the RSS and to provide clearly that persons believing in or resorting to violence and secret methods will have no place in the Sangh. The RSS leader has also clarified that the constitution will be worked on a democratic basis.

Further:

> In the light of the modifications made and clarifications given by the RSS leader, the Government of India have come to the conclusion that the RSS organization should be *given an opportunity* to function as a democratic, cultural organization owing loyalty to the Indian Constitution and recognizing the National Flag eschewing secrecy and abjuring violence.[3]

The assurance has been cynically flouted.

The RSS was accused even by Sardar Patel – who would have liked it to join the Congress – of spreading 'communal poison'. He wrote to Golwalkar on September 11, 1948: 'As a final result of the poison, the country had to suffer the sacrifice of the invaluable life of Gandhiji. Even an iota of the sympathy of the Government or of the people no more remained for the RSS. In fact opposition grew. Opposition turned more severe, when the RSS men expressed joy and distributed sweets after Gandhiji's death.' Gopal Godse later revealed that 'all the brothers were in the RSS, Nathuram, Dattatreya, myself and Govind.' Nathuram, the assassin, 'did not leave the RSS.' L.K. Advani's disclaimer of the Godse–RSS link reflected 'cowardice', Gopal Godse said (*Frontline*, January 28, 1994).

The Nehru–Patel rift on the RSS continued to haunt Indian politics and the RSS profited by the ambiguity. To Patel, the RSS men were 'patriots who love the country' (January 6, 1948). His letters to Golwalkar were warm ('Brother Golwalkar'), even after his arrest, in contrast to Nehru's curtness. In the very letter in which he condemned the RSS, Patel told Golwalkar that 'The RSS men can carry on their patriotic endeavour only by joining the Congress.' Golwalkar was willing (November 5, 1948) to collaborate – as he put it, Congress 'in the political field' and RSS 'in the cultural field'. But he refused to merge the two. In 1950–51, Shyama Prasad Mookerjee accepted those very terms to set up the Jan Sangh.

On October 7, 1949, during Nehru's absence abroad, Patel was able to get the Congress Working Committee to open the Congress membership to RSS men. Nehru had the decision rescinded after his return on November 7. RSS men could join the Congress only if they gave up its membership. It is a measure of Patel's softness for the RSS that he should have gone so far despite the fact that even while the correspondence was on, Golwalkar 'tried to smuggle out of jail two letters in order to get the [RSS] Satyagraha campaign restarted.' Patel complained to D.P. Mishra about Golwalkar 'abusing confidence'.

It is also a measure of the depth of Nehru's commitment to secularism – and of his foresight – that he refused to have anything to do with the RSS. 'I remember Bapu telling me after his first meeting with Golwalkar that he was partly impressed by him *but at the same time did not trust him*. After his second or third meeting he expressed a very strong opinion against Golwalkar and the RSS and said that it was impossible to rely upon their word. They appear to be highly reasonable when talked to but they had no compunction in acting in exact contradiction to what they said. My own impression has been the same', Nehru wrote to Patel on October 27, 1948.[4]

THE EMERGENCY AND AFTER

It was Jayaprakash Narayan's tragedy that, while he shared Nehru's outlook, he adopted Patel's attitude in a moment of crisis. JP was cynically betrayed by the RSS and died a disillusioned man. At the Second National Conference Against Communalism held in New Delhi in January 1968, JP had said, 'The secular protestations of the Jan Sangh will never be taken seriously unless it cuts the bonds that tie it firmly to the RSS machine. Nor can the RSS be treated as a cultural organization as long as it remains the mentor and effective manipulator of a political party.'

Six years later JP accepted support from both during his struggle against Indira Gandhi's corrupt government. During the Emergency, the RSS Chief Deoras wrote cringing letters from prison to Prime Minister Indira Gandhi, Maharashtra Chief Minister S.B. Chavan, and to Vinoba Bhave. They were placed on the table of the Maharashtra Assembly on October 18, 1977. He wrote to the Prime Minister, first, on August 22 congratulating her on her speech on Independence day ('balanced and befitting to the occasion') and begged of her to lift the ban on the RSS. He next congratulated her 'as five judges of the Supreme Court have upheld the validity of your election' (November 11, 1975). She had won the case, not on merit, but by an utterly immoral amendment of the law with retrospective effect. The plea for release of RSS detenues and lifting the ban was repeated. *He did not, however, plead for a lifting of the Emergency nor for the release of all the detenues. He said that the RSS 'has no connection with these movements' in Bihar and Gujarat.* The RSS was later to claim the opposite. Deoras ended by offering the services of 'lakhs of RSS volunteers . . . for the national upliftment (Government as well as non-Government).' This offer was made during the Emergency to a dictator to legitimize her rule. Indira Gandhi ignored the offer of a deal whereupon Deoras wrote yet another letter (July 16, 1976) congratulating her, this time, for 'your efforts to improve relations with Pakistan and China are also praiseworthy' – a policy he would have denounced if he were free. His letter to Vinoba Bhave explicitly expressed the RSS's willingness 'to participate in the *planned programme* of action relating to the country's progress and prosperity under the leadership of the Prime Minister.'

In all his letters Deoras was concerned about the RSS alone. *Not once did he ask for the release of all detenues or lifting of Emergency.* Copies of these letters were received in jail and demoralized the RSS detenues. Madhu Limaye spent 19 months in three jails which were in RSS areas and knew of the RSS detenues' letters of apology. Baba Udhav, the labour leader of Pune, testified: 'Written queries were circulated in the Yeravada Central Jail three or four times asking detenues if they would be prepared to sign an undertaking. I have seen with my own eyes majority of the RSS detenues signing their assent to do so' (*Janata*, September 16, 1979). The RSS organ *Panchjanya* enthusiastically welcomed Sanjay Gandhi's entry into politics (December 21, 1975) and praised him more than once. So did *Tarun Bharat* of Pune.

Once the Emergency was over, JP tried to retrieve the position. Madhu Limaye reported to him of his discussions with Deoras and secured JP's approval. The problem was two-fold – opening of the RSS to non-Hindus and 'the formation of an integrated volunteer organization' which, while autonomous, would have 'friendly relations' with the Janata. The RSS rejected both. Limaye had only to publish this on August 2, 1977 when the RSS General Secretary flatly denied any understanding on relations with the Janata Party.

At this point JP made his position public. In an interview with *Samayika Varta*, a weekly, he said that there was no justification for the RSS to continue as a separate body. 'I have noticed a change in their outlook. They no longer have a feeling of animosity towards other communities. But in their hearts of hearts they still believe in the concept of Hindu Rashtra.' Muley wrote to JP (September 23, 1977) expressing his 'bewilderment'. The RSS would continue as before to espouse the Hindu Rashtra ideal.

JP and Deoras met twice on October 30 and November 1, 1977 but it was too late to change the RSS. Deoras had skillfully bought time when the pressure was greatest *immediately after the 1977 elections*. In March and April 1977 he had repeatedly expressed willingness to consider membership of non-Hindus in the RSS.

On March 28, 1977 Deoras said that the 'long awaited moment' had come to consider the question of widening the membership of the movement. On April 11 he went further in hinting at change. There had been a sea change in the attitude of RSS workers because they had shared experiences with Jamaat-e-Islami workers in jail. He even went so far as to declare that the doors of the RSS would be opened for Muslims; but a decision had yet to be taken. On June 27 the RSS general body, the Pratinidhi Sabha, played for time: the 'highly sensitive problem has to be tackled with care and caution'.

Deoras blandly told JP that 'Hindu and Bharatiya' were synonymous and the RSS was seriously considering the minorities' membership but 'undue haste would not help.' JP addressed an RSS camp (November 3, 1977) and even praised it as 'a revolutionary organization . . . there is no other organization in the country which can match you.' He gently counselled 'basic change in the role of the Sangh' and 'a modification in its aims and objectives. Though it is not a reality even the people identify it with Hindu communal and caste interests.'

On April 8, 1979, *Dinman*, a Hindi weekly, published the draft of a letter from JP to Prime Minister Morarji Desai which he had proposed to send before he fell ill and was removed to hospital in Bombay on March 18. *Dinman's* correspondent had met JP in Patna. The text is set out in full:

> Some friends have repeatedly complained that the Rashtriya Swayamsevak Sangh is making efforts to grab the leadership in the Government. *Like other political parties the RSS is free to influence politics and it is doing so.* But my only objection is that the RSS people are trying to *influence politics under the garb of a cultural organization.* I have advised the leaders of the RSS to merge themselves with organizations sympathetic to them or get affiliated with the Janata Party. But, they declined my advice on the plea that they have nothing to do with politics. *I absolutely do not agree with this logic of the RSS.* I still feel that the RSS should merge itself with the pro-Janata organizations. But if it is bent upon retaining its own distinct identity I would then repeat that it should include in it non-Hindus – Muslims, Christians, etc. *I have always condemned Hindu nationalism of the RSS.* For it is a dangerous doctrine and is against the ideal of *composite Indian nationalism.* In democracy every organization has a right to propagate its philosophy or ideology – this is essence of democracy. But when it aspires to dominate politics, we would have to be careful to see whether such philosophy or ideology threatens the basic philosophy of Indian nationalism. I have no quarrel with the association of the RSS with the Janata Party. But *it will have to give up its Hindu image and become completely secular.* If it does not do so, it should keep its hands off politics, and snap its ties with every faction of the Janata Party.
>
> But as Prime Minister of India, it is your duty to make efforts to improve the RSS or make it a secular force. *Its efforts to upset the secular basis of Indian nationalism and the government should be opposed by all thinking individuals.*

Dinman also quoted JP as having said verbally: 'Every time the RSS people assure me that they would internally improve. But I do not know what do they do after going from here. It is continuing like this for the last four years. After all there is a limit to every thing.' (*Janata*, May 13, 1979).

JP was right. On July 8, 1976, for instance, leaders of the Opposition parties had met in New Delhi. Para 4 of the minutes read:

'Choudhary Charan Singh raised the question of the RSS. He stated his firm belief that no RSS volunteers can join the new party and no member of the new party can join the RSS. It was a question of dual membership which could not be allowed and there should be no scope in the new party for surreptitious work.' It was a direct challenge. O.P. Tyagi spoke for the Jan Sangh: 'Shri Tyagi said that the new party can lay down whatever conditions it sees fit. Currently the RSS was banned and it stood dissolved.'[5] A year later the RSS and the Jan Sangh leaders resiled from this assurance.

In December 1977 they objected to an amendment to Clause V of the Janata Constitution which would have denied membership to anyone who was a member of 'any other organization whose aims, objectives and activities are inconsistent with those of the Janata Party'. At Morarji Desai's instance a decision was put off. Only three months later, on March 6, 1978, as we have seen, the RSS revealed its true self in the Nagpur Court.

After the Janata Government's fall in July 1979, the Party amended Clause V, to declare that 'the concept of a religious state is against the creed of the Janata Party'. Its President Chandrashekhar negotiated a formula with Deoras whereby, like office bearers of the parties, legislators would also be debarred from taking part in 'day-to-day RSS activities.' It was to be confirmed by the RSS Pratinidhi Sabha in March 1980. Chandrashekhar and Rajendra Singh announced the accord separately on July 24, 1979.

When the RSS Executive met on March 23, 1980, Singh apprised it 'of the circumstances and spirit in which his statement of July 24, 1979 was made. After due consideration the ABKM [the Executive] felt that nothing need be done in the matter. The Pratinidhi Sabha endorsed the decision unanimously.' In February 1980 the Janata Party Executive had adopted the agreed formula as a basis for discussion with the Jan Sangh faction. It said: 'No legislator or office-bearer of the Janata Party shall participate in the day-to-day activities of the RSS. No member of the Janata Party shall work in any front organization which functions in competition to one sponsored by the Janata Party.'

On March 18, the Janata Parliamentary Board adopted this formulation. The Jan Sangh accepted its second part, but not the first. The issue was remitted to the National Executive which was to meet on April 3. Before it could meet on March 26, the Jan Sangh called a Convention of its supporters on April 5, 1980.

On April 4, the National Executive adopted the Parliamentary Board's formulation by 17 votes as against 14 for Morarji's formula which the Jan Sangh had accepted. His text read: 'Every member of the Janata Party shall unconditionally accept and strive to preserve *the composite culture and secular state established in our country and nation not based on religion.* He shall not allow his membership of any other organization to derogate from this obligation.' The National Executive further decided that:

1. No member of the Janata Party shall work in any front organizations which function in competition to any organization sponsored by the Janata Party.

2. No member of what are described as constituent parties of the Janata Party should hold exclusive meetings of their own or take any action calculated to capture the elected organs of the party.

The next day the Jan Sangh decided to form a new Party, the Bharatiya Janata Party (BJP). A futile effort to paper the cracks had ended.

The BJP lost no time in demonstrating that it was the same old BJS anew. 'I have a number of old friends in Jana Sangh, people came to see me asking for my mediation for various things', Golwalkar acknowledged in February 1971. Two Presidents of the Jan Sangh had to quit the Party because of the RSS's domination, Pandit Mauli Chandra Sharma and Balraj Madhok. Atal Behari Vajpayee's assurance on November 6, 1977 that the Jan Sangh members of the Janata Party had 'given up old beliefs' was an admission of their incompatibility with Janata Party's credo. Non-Hindus could object to the RSS flag, prayer and many such things. Deoras deliberately refused to change. Vajpayee tried to stall but, as ever, gave in.

Vajpayee said: 'Personally, I feel that the RSS should open its doors to all Indians irrespective of religion. But the RSS says that it is trying to serve the Hindu society . . . they have changed and they will have to change much more.' (*Sunday*, March 15, 1979). Next came the famous article in *Indian Express* (August 2, 1979). Referring to the 'RSS bogey', he wrote:

the RSS, claiming to be a social and cultural organization should have taken greater pains to demonstrate that they did not seek a political role. Patronizing a press that takes sides in the sordid politics of power, involvement in youth bodies that interact with political parties, participating in trade union rivalries such as the one which recently brought enormous misery to the people of Delhi by callously cutting off the water supply – these do not help an organization to establish its apolitical credentials.

It is possible that some people genuinely feel apprehensive about the RSS. A certain onus accordingly devolved on the RSS, an onus that has not been discharged effectively by the RSS. Its repudiation of the theocratic form of the State was welcome, yet the question could legitimately be asked – why does it not open its doors to non-Hindus? Recent statements of the RSS Chief, Mr Deoras, indicate that non-Hindus are being encouraged to join the organization. A national corollary of this process would be clear enunciation by the RSS that by 'Hindu Rashtra' it means the Indian nation which includes non-Hindus as equal members.

The other course of action open to the RSS could be to function only as a Hindu religious-cum-social-cultural organization wedded to the task of eradicating the evils prevailing in Hindu society and revitalizing it to face the challenge of modern times. The kind of selfless service that the RSS has rendered in times of natural calamities has endeared it even to its critics and has established beyond doubt its capacity for constructive work for ameliorating the suffering of those who are in need of help. Such an organization will draw support and sustenance from members of various political parties as has been the case with institutions like the Arya Samaj.

Soon after, on December 18 he advised the RSS to change its 'methodology, ideology, programme and activities', replace the 'Hindu Rashtra' ideal with 'Bharat Rashtra', and 'clarify its role'. He noted that the RSS had not undergone any change although he and others had advised its leadership on two different occasions, in 1948 and in 1977. In August 1983 he again came back to the issue. This time Deoras reacted, swiftly and sneeringly: the terms India and Hindu are synonymous, 'but if anybody wants to change it because he is ashamed of the word "Hindu" we cannot accept the suggestion. . . . Those who want to water down the Hindu character of India are also playing with our liberal traditions.'

THE QUESTION OF VIOLENCE

The country has suffered for the compromises some made with the RSS. Its conduct is as vile as its pronouncements are poisonous. The hate it exudes leads inescapably to violence. The RSS *believes* in the use of violence. It is part of its credo.

On June 11, 1970, Golwalkar waxed eloquent before a group of journalists. The communal atmosphere was tense in the wake of the Ahmedabad and Bhiwandi riots. *Organiser* reported this exchange:

> *Q.* Who will teach Muslims to identify themselves completely with the country and its culture?
> *A.* You and me, all of us.
> *Q.* Can you teach by beating?
> *A.* Beating is of two kinds: mother beating her child and an enemy sticking a man. We have not done any beating. But if, as and when we do teach by beating, it will be like the mother's beating of her child – out of love and solicitude for the child's welfare.

Yet, he complained 'misunderstandings are sought to be created about the training in the use of *danda* (lathi), *yogchap* (lesim), *khadga* (sword), *vetracharma* (canefight) etc. that is imparted in the RSS branches.' 'What has our good behaviour towards Muslim faith and the Muslim people brought us?' Golwalkar asked. The alternative is propounded openly.

> Is there any place for violence in the life of a society? Yes, but it should be used as a surgeon's knife . . . to cure society of any malady that needs such a surgical intervention. . . . In this task of self-protection we might have to destroy evil persons. . . . If these *Asur* [evil forces] are to be defeated through the use of force, force should be used. . . . Generally speaking, it is a matter of common experience that evil forces do not understand the language of logic and sweet nature. They can be controlled by force.

The record of the RSS has been a gory one. And it has uttered one lie after another to cover it.

'In none of the court judgements or in the Report of any Commission of Inquiry appointed by the Government has it been said that *the volunteers of the Sangh were involved*' Deoras wrote to Indira Gandhi on August 22, 1975. More brazenly, he claimed in

November 1979: 'Indira Gandhi has also said that no enquiry commission appointed during her rule even [*sic*] has found the RSS guilty of inciting communal disturbances.' He could not have been unaware of the fact that in her famous speech in the Lok Sabha on July 22, 1975 she quoted from such Reports while denouncing the RSS. And there are a good number of them.

Justice P. Jaganmohan Reddy of the Supreme Court headed the Commission of Inquiry into the communal disturbances at Ahmedabad and other places in Gujarat, on and after September 18, 1969. Its Report noted that 'The agitation had received the blessing of the local Bharatiya Jan Sangh workers who did not want to involve themselves directly but suggested the formation of an organization known as Hindu Dharma Raksha Samiti with Harischandra Panchal, an old RSS worker, as its convenor.' The Commission found that the Hindu Dharma Raksha Samiti had issued pamphlets calling on the Hindus 'to prepare for "Dharma Yudha" without waiting for justice to be done by the Government, to sever all economic and social relations with the community that has attacked their religion, viz. the Muslims.' The Report noted 'the definite part played in various Districts which were affected by the workers of the Jan Sangh and Hindu Mahasabha organizations or by persons having leanings towards them. There is evidence definitely that they took a leading part in the Districts of Amreli, Banaskantha, Mehsana, and Baroda.'

United front tactics were used in the Bhiwandi and Jalgaon riots as well. There was the Rashtriya Utsav Mandal in the former and the Shree Ram Tarun Mandal in the latter. A Commission of Inquiry consisting of Justice D.P. Madon (later of the Supreme Court), found that 'the guiding spirit of the RUM was Dr Vyas, President of the Bhiwandi Branch of Jan Sangh. The majority of its members belonged to the Jan Sangh or were from Jan Sangh', apart from some who belonged to the Shiv Sena.

The Madon Commission took note of Golwalkar's speeches:

In India there should be the rule of the Hindus. There cannot be a good administration if there is the rule of various people like Hindus, Muslims, Christians, Parsis, etc. If there is the head of an ass attached to the body of a monkey it will not work well. Such a body will be attacked by worms and will emit bad smells. Similarly, any administration by different types of people will not work well. It will lack in morality, character and culture. . . .

In two other reports even the Jan Sangh cover could not conceal the RSS. The Report of the Justice Vithayathil Commission of Inquiry on the Tellicherry riots in December 1971 said:

> I have no doubt that the RSS had taken an active part in rousing up anti-Muslim feeling among the Hindus of Tellicherry and in preparing the background for the disturbances. The same can be said about the Jan Sangh also. Although there may not be any official connection between the Jan Sangh and the RSS, *the RSS is generally regarded as the military wing of the Jan Sangh and the Jan Sangh, the political wing of the RSS.* That the two organizations are regarded as one by the common people is admitted by P13W1 Chandrasekharan . . . the Jan Sangh unit in Kerala has taken the same attitude towards the Muslims as the RSS.

Chandrasekharan was the Secretary of the Hindus Samekhsana Samiti ' – another united front – and a prominent RSS worker in Tellicherry'.

The Report of the Justice Jitendra Narain Commission of Inquiry into the Jamshedpur riots in April 1979 has one chapter that deals with the RSS. Deoras addressed an RSS Conference on April 1, 1979, just ten days before the outbreak of the disturbances. The Report observed that 'his speech amounted to communal propaganda' and held the RSS responsible for creating a climate for the disturbances that took place. The Commission also concluded that a certain Dina Nath Pandey was

> a member of the RSS, his actions followed a line which was in fulfillment of the general scheme of the Hindu Communalists of Jamshedpur and that they were also aimed at achieving the plan announced in the leaflet circulated by them. His conduct had, thus, directly contributed to the outbreak of the riot at Jamshedpur, on the occasion of the Ram Navami festival of 1979.

There is also Justice Venugopal's Report on the Kanyakumari riots of 1982, indicting the RSS severely for its role in fomenting riots against the Christians. There is also the Report of the Commission of Inquiry on the Bhagalpur riots of 1989 published in 1995.

The joint Report by Justices R.C. Sinha and S. Shamsul Hasan of the Patna High Court on the Bhagalpur riots also censured the Sangh *parivar*. The riots had erupted on October 24, 1989, when a

Ramshila procession 'organized by the BJP, VHP and RSS' wended its way through a Muslim locality. In March 1989 Deoras had addressed a meeting there, in which he tried to arouse Hindu sentiment. A thousand lives were lost, 900 of them being Muslims. The Chairman, Justice R.N. Prasad exonerated the *parivar*. His daughter, Reeta Verma, was a BJP Member of Parliament.

Two features stand out in all the riots – RSS men deliberately march in a procession through Muslim areas shouting offensive slogans and the slightest response is seized as pretext to launch pre-planned attacks. This explains why Ashok Singhal of the VHP said, in the presence of Advani, in New Delhi on April 4 1991: 'Our shobha yatras (religious processions) should pass through every locality.' This was the technique used by fascists in London in the 1930s when they would march through Jewish areas.

These are the findings of commissions of inquiry set up by law. There are, besides, reports of investigations by academics and journalists of repute. *The Statesman* blamed the RSS and the Jan Sangh's workers for building up the tension before the Rourkela riots in 1964. On January 1, 1969 *Indian Express* carried a detailed report on the RSS which noted 'the growth of the RSS has coincided with the recent wave of communal riots in the country.' There are well authenticated reports about the RSS's guilt in the Biharsharif riots in 1981. Its misdeeds in Assam and in the South have been well documented.

Strangely, the Indira Gandhi–Golwalkar correspondence went unnoticed. At the end of the Bangladesh war, Golwalkar wrote (December 22, 1971): 'The biggest measure of credit for this achievement goes to you.' She replied on January 13, 1972 thanking him for 'your good wishes' and throwing a broad hint that 'it is in the interest of the nation to preserve this unity.' Golwalkar replied (January 19): 'It is true that feeling of unity should always be present in the nation. Everyone has to know his responsibility and endeavour to this end.' Golwalkar's successor, Deoras, not only advised the Janata to 'forgive and forget' (May 5, 1977) but on Indira Gandhi's return to power, he said on February 12, 1980 that there was 'every possibility' of the RSS cooperating with the Congress (I). Indira Gandhi had 'changed' and ideologically there was no difference with the Congress (I). On Sanjay Gandhi's death, Deoras said that 'he had made a powerful impact on national politics. That was not merely because of his family connections but also because of his individual qualities and personality.' *Organiser* approvingly described Indira Gandhi as a 'Political Hindu' (July 3, 1983).

Collaboration, for the RSS, is nothing new. A Bombay Home Department report on the Quit India Movement noted that 'the Sangh has scrupulously kept itself within the law, and, in particular has refrained from taking any part in the disturbances that broke out in August 1942'. It obeyed the colonial government's orders and survived.

The RSS counterparts elsewhere, like the John Birch Society in the United States are at the lunatic fringe. Not so in India. Here, the RSS has floated a political party and deceived many by its double-talk again and again. Intellectually, its idiom and ideas are sterile and revivalist. It is not interested in social reform. Its outlook on women – membership is confined to males – and on caste is retrograde.

'Even the saints cannot be said to be above politics' Rajendra Singh had said (March 12, 1978). Politics has always been the RSS's prime concern. In 2000 it occupies the centrestage in Indian politics. This is where repeated compromises by democrats with a viciously fascist force have brought us.

3

THE SANGH PARIVAR
AND THE BRITISH

Shyama Prasad Mookerjee, the founder of the Jan Sangh and patron saint of the BJP, was quite clear in his mind as to how the Government should respond, if the Congress gave a call to the British rulers to Quit India. In a letter to the Governor of Bengal, on July 26, 1942 – less than a fortnight before the All India Congress Committee passed the Quit India resolution on August 8 – he wrote: 'Let me now refer to the situation that may be created in the province as a result of any widespread movement launched by the Congress. Anybody, who during the war, plans to stir up *mass feelings*, resulting in internal disturbances or *insecurity*, must be resisted by any Government that may function for *the time being*.'[1] Note that he was not against acts of violence alone. He was against what the British rulers dubbed 'sedition'. He was against arousal of 'mass feelings' which led to 'insecurity' in the regime as distinct from ('or') internal disturbances.

Mookerjee knew whom he was writing to when he provided his unsolicited advice. It was the iron-fisted Sir John Herbert. Against this explicit advice to such a man, qualifications like 'mere repression is not remedy' were pointless and for the record. As the historian Sumit Guha recalled in an article, 'The Governor, Sir John Herbert, felt he knew best. On August 9, he summoned the Haq Ministry and told its members to endorse the Government crackdown or resign. Nobody resigned, and a brutal campaign of repression was launched' (*IE* August 17, 1992).

Mookerjee was then Finance Minister in the Bengal government headed by a member of the Muslim League, Fazlul Haq, who had broken from it – only to rejoin it later. That was the day – August 9 – when Mookerjee should have resigned. He did not, hoping that the Governor would make a deal with him on power-sharing as proposed in his letter. It expressed Mookerjee's 'sense of loyalty to my leader', Fazlul Haq, and made a concrete proposal:

> The question is how to combat this movement [Quit India] in Bengal? The administration of the province should be carried on in such a manner that *in spite of the best efforts of the Congress, this movement will fail to take root in the province*. It should be possible for us, specially responsible Ministers, to be able to tell the public that the freedom for which the Congress has started the movement, already belongs to the representatives of the people. *In some spheres it might be limited during the emergency. Indians have to trust the British*, not for the sake of Britain, not for any advantage that the British might gain, but for the maintenance of the defence and freedom of the province itself. You, as Governor, will function as the constitutional head of the province and will be guided entirely on the advice of your Ministers.

In other words, if the British transferred power to the Haq–Mookerjee rump, Mookerjee was more than willing to continue as Minister though the Congress leaders, MLAs and rank and file were behind bars. He resigned on November 16, 1942 and trotted out in his letter of resignation a whole set of belated prevarication on why he did not resign when, in his own conscience, he ought to have. He had written to the Viceroy on August 12 and received a reply in 'early September'. Explanations of the two months' delay were few and laboured. The talk of a 'settlement' was disingenuous. For, his proposal to the British for power-sharing was made in a specific context mentioned at the very outset – 'The question is how to *combat* this movement in Bengal', i.e., 'combat' the Quit India movement.

Mookerjee began his political career in 1929 when he was elected to the Bengal Legislative Council from the University constituency – as a *Congress* candidate. He was again elected to the Assembly in

1937 from the same constituency. In February 1939 V.D. Savarkar toured Bengal. Mookerjee was 'a discovery of Savarkar's tour in Bengal,' writes Savarkar's biographer, Dhananjay Keer. It was only in May 1937 that the newly-elected Congress Government of Bombay removed completely the humiliating conditions to which Savarkar had submitted in order to secure his release from prison.[2]

The release order issued by the Governor exercising the power conferred on him by Section 401 of the Code of Criminal Procedure, 1898, reads as follows:

> (1) That the said Vinayak Damodar Savarkar will reside within the territories administered by the Governor of Bombay in Council and within the Ratnagiri District within the said territories, and will not go beyond the limits of that district without the permission of Government, or in case of urgency, of the District Magistrate. (2) That he will not engage publicly or privately in any manner of political activities without the consent of Government for a period of five years, such restriction being renewable at the discretion of Government at the expiry of the said term.

Savarkar accepted these conditions without any compunction. The Government suggested that he should state that his trial was fair and the sentence awarded was just. At the same time, it told him this was 'in no way made a condition of his release'. Yet, he went ahead and made this statement: 'I hereby acknowledge that I had a fair trial and just sentence. I heartily abhor methods of violence resorted to in days gone by, and I feel myself duty bound to uphold Law and the Constitution to the best of my powers and am willing to make the Reform a success in so far as I may be allowed to do so in future.'

The reference to the Reform here is to the Montagu-Chelmsford proposals of 1919 which fell woefully short of Indian hopes and expectations and were rejected by all sections of Indians.

Savarkar became president of the Hindu Mahasabha immediately thereafter. Mookerjee was his prize catch.

The Congress historian, Pattabhi Sitaramayya, recorded that

> on the day of the arrests of Gandhi and his colleagues, Savarkar's call to the Hindus was one of 'no support to the Congress move'. There was nothing in it to be surprised at. All along he has preached the gospel of Hindutva, Hindu communalism, not Indian nationalism. In the

formation of Ministries in Muslim-majority provinces while the
Congress [leadership] was in prison, he encouraged Hindu participation
in them in different provinces on different grounds . . .[3]

He proceeded to mention how, only a few months after his resignation
from the Bengal Cabinet, Mookerjee's interest in regaining his job
revived.

> This revival of interest not in elections but in the formation of Ministries
> while the Congress was in duress, sounds strange, indeed; not because
> it was rooted in any intrinsic strength of the Sabha but because it was
> traceable to an unholy and an uncouth [sic] combination with the
> opponents of the Congress. The sad fate of the Sabha candidates during
> the General Elections of 1937 is well known. Nor has the Sabha run
> any of its candidates at the time of the by-elections.[4]

*This very fact that the Mahasabha had no roots in popular support
drove Mookerjee to try to strike a deal over the heads of the people
with the British rulers.* The Congress leadership, in Bengal and at
the Central level, had done little to satisfy his ambitions. Savarkar
did.

Sitaramayya supported his charge by citing another fact which
sounds incredible today. *The Hindu Mahasabha was in a coalition
Government with the Muslim League in Sind.* Though the Sind
Assembly passed a resolution endorsing the demand for Pakistan,
the Mahasabha Ministers did not resign from the Government but
'contented themselves with a protest', for the record.[5]

Mahasabha president Savarkar issued an edict on September
1942: 'I issue this definite instruction to all Hindu Sabhaites in
particular and all Hindu Sangathanists in general . . . holding any
post or position of vantage in the Government services should stick
to them and continue to perform their regular duties.' This was
dutifully followed. So much so that, according to an intelligence report
of June 10, 1943, when Aruna Asaf Ali pleaded with her friend Sarla,
daughter of Sir Jwala Prasad Srivastava, a member of the Viceroy's
Executive Council, to 'force her father to resign on the issue of
Gandhi's fast . . . Sarla replied that as her father has taken the line of
Hindu Mahasabha, he could not follow her advice.'[6]

Indeed, the Mahasabha's working committee had passed a
resolution on August 31, 1942 asking all Mahasabhaites to remain at

their jobs. Savarkar's edict was follow-up to it. So much for the
Mahasabha. What of the RSS? It must be borne in mind that in the
first half of the 1940s, the Mahasabha loomed larger on the political
horizon than did the RSS. Ego clashes between Savarkar and
Golwalkar strained relations at times. The relationship is described
in detail by Walter K. Andersen and Shridhar D. Damle in their superb
work *The Brotherhood in Saffron*.

It was G.D. (alias Babarao) Savarkar, elder brother of Vinayak,
who helped the RSS to expand into western Maharashtra. Savarkar
was close to the RSS founder K.B. Hedgewar but had 'disdain for
Golwalkar . . . Both men were apprehensive regarding the other's
role in the Hindu unification movement.' Eventually, as we know,
Savarkar emerged discredited despite his acquittal in the Gandhi
assassination case. His favourite pupil Mookerjee strayed into the RSS
camp and was made its captive. After his death in June 1953, the RSS
lost no time in completing its grip over the Jan Sangh. This grip holds
the BJP leaders – far smaller men than Mookerjee – completely in its
thrall.

To revert to the RSS's role in the early 1940s, Andersen and Damle
record:

> Golwalkar believed that the British not be given any excuse to ban the
> RSS. When the British banned military drill and the use of uniforms in
> all non-official organizations, the RSS complied. On April 29, 1943,
> Golwalkar distributed a circular to senior RSS figures, announcing the
> termination of the RSS military department. The wording of the circular
> reveals his apprehensions regarding the possibility of a ban on the RSS:
> 'We discontinued practices included in the Government's early order
> on military drill and uniforms . . . to keep our work clearly within bounds
> of law, as every law abiding institution should. . . . Hoping that
> circumstances would ease early, we had in a sense only suspended that
> part of our training. Now, however, we decide to stop it altogether and
> abolish the department without waiting for the time to change.'
>
> Golwalkar was not a revolutionary in the conventional sense of the
> term. The British understood this. In an official report on RSS activity
> prepared in 1943, the Home Department concluded that 'it would
> be difficult to argue that the RSS constitutes an immediate menace
> to law and order . . . ' Commenting on the violence that accompanied
> the 1942 Quit India Movement, the Bombay Home Department

observed: 'The Sangh has scrupulously kept itself within the law, and in particular, has refrained from taking part in the disturbances that broke out in August, 1942 . . .'

The Mahasabha and the RSS merged in the person of Gandhiji's assassin, Nathuram Godse. Not surprisingly. The RSS apologists would have us believe that he was not a member of RSS but was only a Mahasabhaite and a follower of Savarkar. That, he was, but more, besides. Godse said in court: 'Millions of Hindu Sanghathanists looked up to him [V.D. Savarkar] as the chosen hero, as the ablest and most faithful advocate of the Hindu cause. I too was one of them.' The whole truth emerged 46 years later, in December 1993, with the publication of the assassin's brother Gopal's book *Why I Assassinated Mahatma Gandhi*. Speaking in New Delhi on the occasion of the release of his book, Gopal Godse said that he and his brother had been active members of the RSS (*TS* December 24, 1993).

In 1939 Jinnah propounded the poisonous two-nation theory and demanded, in 1940, the country's partition. Savarkar had propounded the theory in his book *Hindutva*, a decade and a half earlier.

In 1942 Shyama Prasad Mookerjee made a bid for power by a deal with the British in order to install Hindu Raj. His innermost thoughts, bared to the pages of his *Diary*, expose the *parivar's* motivations and also illustrate the central problem of all plural societies: 'As seventy-five per cent of the population were Hindus, and if India was to adopt a democratic form of government, the Hindus would automatically play a major role in it' (p. 106). He and his political heirs sought to utilize that vote for the ends of power using the Hindutva card.

4

THE RSS AND GANDHI

Were Mahatma Gandhi alive to hear the paeans which the Rashtriya Swayamsevak Sangh (RSS) and the Bharatiya Janata Party (BJP) so lustily sing in his praise today, he might have exclaimed in this couplet written by his erstwhile colleague, Maulana Mohammed Ali:

Jeete jee to kuch na dikhlaya magar
Mar ke Jauhar aap ke jauhar khile.
(You never revealed anything of yourself while you were alive
The gem that was you, Jauhar, shone after your death.)

Four features that no serious student of public affairs should overlook mark the Sangh *parivar's* current stance on Gandhi. There were stray references in the past but the enthusiasm is recent, sudden, orchestrated and motivated. One has only to read RSS supremo Rajendra Singh's speech on Vijayadashmi day 1997 to be struck by this (*Organiser* October 26). It begins with homage to Ram (one paragraph), followed by remembrance of the founder Hedgewar (one paragraph), and praise of Mahatma Gandhi (two exuberant paragraphs). But he is dropped as the orator warms up to his un-Gandhian themes. Hedgewar dominates as does Ram, but only in the context of Ayodhya.

Rajendra Singh launched the campaign on October 2, 1997, Gandhi's birth anniversary, and hoped to lead it to a climax on January

30, 1998, the 50th anniversary of Gandhi's tragic assassination. On October 2, he addressed a mammoth rally of RSS cadres, at which Atal Behari Vajpayee was also present, and waxed eloquent on Gandhi. Earlier, BJP president L.K. Advani had also discovered rare qualities in Gandhi during his Swarna Jayanthi Rath Yatra to celebrate 50 years of Independence. There was, however, no reference to Gandhian teachings in the four-day training camp of the BJP at Jhinjauli in Haryana. It was the 'Thought of Deen Dayal Upadhyaya', a president of the Jan Sangh, the BJP's ancestor, which was propagated (*TT* September 4, 1997). In public, on October 2, Rajendra Singh used language never heard from those quarters: 'Gandhiji is one of the shining *navratnas* [nine gems] among the sons of Bharatmata,' adding: 'He is held in reverence by the [*sic*] society *though not decorated by the Government with Bharat Ratna*' a cheap bid to score over others and emerge as Gandhi loyalists. Incongruously, the other topics he covered were Ayodhya, Kashi, Mathura and Swadeshi. The RSS announced on October 8, 1997 the launch of a mass-contact programme, commencing from January 12, on 'Swadeshi'.

By now, the derision which these antics had aroused was beginning to tell on the *parivar's* nerves. The BJP's general secretary, Sushma Swaraj, angrily declared on October 17, 1997 that 'Mahatma Gandhi is not the monopoly of the Congress party.' This was in reference to Congress president Sitaram Kesri's jibe that the BJP was trying to 'hijack' Gandhi. By itself, her statement is very true. Only the issue is not one of anyone 'monopolizing' a national hero but of a political movement opposing him ferociously while he lived, rejecting his ideology for decades and suddenly hailing him as one of the nation's *navratnas*. And all this while *continuing* to espouse a credo fundamentally antithetical to his.

There is nothing genuine or spontaneous about this recent and sudden conversion. The orchestration and timing reveal the motives. The Sangh *parivar* profited enormously by the Partition of India. Gandhi's assassination arrested that trend. The damage caused by this self-inflicted wound has not yet healed. It took the RSS–BJP 30 years to achieve some respectability – thanks to the Emergency – and 40 years to come close to acquiring power at the Centre. That, as Advani never fails to remind us, was due to the Ayodhya campaign. The demolition of the Babri Masjid on December 6, 1992 caused a setback. Yet in 1996 the BJP emerged as the largest single party in the

Lok Sabha only to discover that few were willing to sup with it.

Stigmas can never be wiped out, least of all one that is earned by the assassination of a national hero. Forgiveness can be earned by penitent conduct, of which there is no sign. On October 5, 1997, *Organiser* published an advertisement by a Delhi publisher for six 'Readable Attractive New Books', two of them by Gopal Godse: *Qutab Minar is Vishnu Dhwaja* and *Gandhi Ji's Murderer After*. The third book advertised is *May it Please Your Honour*, the assassin's statement in Court. Another is by the Judge who ordered the locks of the gates to the Babri Masjid opened on February 1, 1986 in flagrant breach of the law. *Organiser* is hardly likely to accept advertisements for books critical of the RSS.

In a remarkable coincidence, irrefutable evidence of 'the RSS connection' with Gandhi's assassination surfaced in recent years – just as it was about to claim the Gandhian heritage. Gopal Godse, brother of Gandhi's assassin Nathuram, published his book, *Why I Assassinated Mahatma Gandhi*, in December 1993. Speaking in New Delhi on the occasion of the release of his book, Gopal Godse revealed what many had suspected – they had both been active members of the RSS (*TS* December 24, 1993). Soon thereafter, in an interview to *Frontline* (January 28, 1994), he provided the details and angrily scotched Advani's attempts to disown them:

All the brothers were in the RSS. Nathuram, Dattatreya, myself and Govind. You can say we grew up in the RSS rather than in our home. It was like a family to us. Nathuram had become a *baudhik karyavah* [intellectual worker] in the RSS. He has said in his statement that he left the RSS. He said it because Golwalkar and the RSS were in a lot of trouble after the murder of Gandhi. But he did not leave the RSS.

Asked about Advani's claim that Nathuram had nothing to do with the RSS, Godse replied: 'I have countered him, saying it is cowardice to say that. You can say that RSS did not pass a resolution, saying, "go and assassinate Gandhi." But you do not disown him [Nathuram]. *The Hindu Mahasabha did not disown him*. In 1944, Nathuram started doing Hindu Mahasabha work when he had been a *baudhik karyavah* in the RSS.'

Two decades after the assassination, the RSS mouthpiece (*Organiser*), then edited by K.R. Malkani could remember Gandhi, on January 11, 1970, only in these terms in its editorial: 'It was in support of Nehru's pro-Pakistan stand that Gandhiji went on fast and, in the process, turned the people's wrath on himself.' So, Nathuram Godse represented 'the people,' and the murder he perpetrated was an expression of 'the people's wrath'. In 1961 Deen Dayal Upadhyaya said: 'With all respect for Gandhiji, let us cease to call him 'Father of the Nation'. If we understand the old basis of nationalism, then it will be clear that it is nothing but Hinduism.'

The Times of India editorially noted on October 17, 1989: 'Mr. Advani, while holding forth on "Bharat Mata", now goes so far as to deny that Mahatma Gandhi was the Father of the Nation.' None should be surprised at a photograph showing the RSS supremo, M.S. Golwalkar, sharing, at Pune in 1952, a platform with V.D. Savarkar, who narrowly escaped conviction in the Gandhi murder case.[1]

NAILING THE LIE

This is not the first time that the Sangh *parivar* has tried to invoke Gandhi's name in order to cover up its politics while rejecting all he stood for. Some years ago, one L.C. Pounj, president of the Vishwa Hindu Parishad of the United Kingdom, handed over to the Indian High Commission a letter 'conveying the views of Hindus' there on the Ayodhya issue. It quoted 'the views expressed by Mahatma Gandhi in the *Navajivan* dated 27-7-1937 on the controversy relating to Sri Ramjanmabhoomi' in the wake of 'the riot of 1934' (*Organiser* September 23, 1990). It was said to support the *parivar's* stand.

Two months later, the BJP got into the act. Its general secretary, Krishan Lal Sharma, wrote to none other than the country's Prime Minister Chandra Shekhar, quoting two paragraphs allegedly written by Gandhi, not in *Navajivan*, but in *Harijan Sewak* of the same date, July 27, 1937. This was reported in *The Times of India* of December 3, 1990. *It is important to note that Sharma claimed that he himself had seen a copy of that Hindi weekly.*

The very next day *The Times of India* published a report by its Research Bureau nailing the lie. Gandhi had written no such article. When confronted with this, Sharma now said he had come to know of the article from a local publication *Vishwas* (Trust) which had 'reproduced' it. Changing his tune, he asserted that the responsibility for verification lay with the Prime Minister. 'It is for the Prime Minister to deny its authenticity. *The Times of India* (December 4, 1990) said:

'Despite repeated requests from *The Times of India* Research Bureau, the BJP central office was unable to produce a copy of the original *Harijan Sewak* or *Navajivan* which, according to them, carried the dubious article.'

Undeterred, Sharma wrote a second letter to the Prime Minister quoting Gandhi, once again, in support of the *parivar's* stand on Babri Masjid. This time he cited Volume 26, page 65 of *The Collected Works of Mahatma Gandhi*. In a reply to a letter of a reader of *Young India* Gandhi was said to have said that he did not think a mosque was sacrosanct if it was built in an unauthorized or forcible manner. The letter was said to have been 'published in the issue of February 5, 1925 and in *Sewak* of June [*sic*] 23, 1950' (*TS* December 6, 1950). As we shall see, this lie was also nailed to the counter. Sharma's assurance to the Prime Minister bears recalling: 'Neither my party nor I am in favour of demolishing any mosque. That is why the BJP president, Mr L.K. Advani, has suggested relocation of the Babri Masjid structure at some other place with honour.' Two years latter, almost to the day, the mosque was demolished in Advani's presence and with his approval.

Ajai and Shakuntala Singh who had 'searched through *The Collected Works of Mahatma Gandhi*, all the ninety volumes' could find no such letter (*Mainstream*, January 12, 1991). They asked Sharma 'or any of the Gandhian scholars' to enlighten them. Another article by Vishnu Nagar in the same issue of *Mainstream* quoted a speech by Gandhi on November 30, 1947 in Delhi, where mosques were being taken over and converted to temples: 'Forcible possession of a mosque disgraces Hinduism and Sikhism. It is the duty of the Hindus to remove the idols from the mosque and repair the damage.' Further: 'By installing idols in the mosques they are desecrating the mosques and also insulting the idols.'[2]

The writers had apparently not noticed two thorough exposures of the lie in *People's Democracy*, December 9, 1990. It recalled that as far back as 1950, Jivanji Desai of the Navajivan Trust, publishers of Gandhi's works, had to debunk an exactly similar claim by one Ramgopal Pandey 'Sharad' of Ayodhya. He had cited an article from *Navajivan* of July 27, 1937 while Sharma had cited one of the same date from *Harijan Sewak*. *The Times of India's* Research Bureau had found that there was no issue of the *Sewak* of that date, the closest ones being those of July 24 and 21, 1937. *Navajivan* had ceased publication in 1932 – which explains why Sharma had shifted ground only to come a cropper once again.

People's Democracy reproduced the text of Desai's article in the *Harijan Sewak* of July 13, 1950 entitled 'Concocted Letter & Article'. Apparently Pandey ('Sharad') had written a book *Shriramjanmabhoomi Virodhiyonke Kala Karnamey* (Black Deeds of the Ramjanmabhoomi Opponents) published by its Sewa Samiti at Ayodhya. He claimed to have written to Gandhi on May 15, 1937, received a reply from Mahadev Desai, 'private secretary,' dated May 20 from Wardha notifying that Gandhi would express his views in the Hindi *Navajivan* or *Harijan*. Sure enough, there came an article in *Navajivan* of July 27, 1937 which Pandey reproduced in full in his book.

Jivanji Desai opined that both Mahadev Desai's letter and the quotation from *Navajivan* article, said to be written by Gandhiji, 'are forged.' No Hindi *Navajivan* existed in 1937. Its Hindi edition was *Harijan Sewak*. Jivanji Desai had gone through the files of *Harijan Sewak* as well as *Harijan* (in English) and found that the alleged article 'is equally concocted and false.' Other details fortified the conclusion. Neither Mahadev Desai nor Gandhi was in Wardha around May 20, 1937 either. They were in Gujarat.

People's Democracy reprinted an article by K.G. Mashruwala, a close associate of Gandhi, in *Harijan* and *Harijan Sewak* of August 19, 1950 and entitled 'Muslims of Ayodhya'. It contains an authoritative and contemporary account of the Masjid's takeover on December 23, 1949 based on Akshya Brahmachari's testimony. It puts paid to the lies retailed about the takeover by the *parivar*. The episode of Gandhi's article reveals the depths of mendacity to which high officials of the BJP can stoop. No apology is forthcoming for it to this day.

CAMPAIGN OF CALUMNY

The BJP had, at its first plenary convention in Bombay on December 28, 1980, affirmed 'Gandhian socialism' as one of its five commitments. It was then struggling for respectability. In October 1985 its National Executive abandoned it but, sensing the reaction, the National Council restored it formally. That was the year after its parliamentary debacle.

Differences between Gandhi and the RSS were profound and

irreconcilable. They disagreed on British rule, the use of violence, on Muslims and, most important of all, on India's composite culture. 'This culture of Delhi belongs to both the Hindus and Muslims and not exclusively to either,' Gandhi said on September 11, 1947 (*CWMG* 89:77). In December 1969 the Jan Sangh said that 'any talk of composite culture' was dangerous. Advani denounced the concept at the BJP's Agra session on April 8, 1988. He had joined the RSS at about the same time as the 'Quit India Movement,' he told Christophe Jaffrelot.[3] Three members of the Viceroy's Executive Council resigned in 1943 when Gandhi went on a fast (N.P. Sarkar, M.S. Aney and Homi Mody). The pro-Hindu Mahasabha, joined the Council. Aney, who was pro-Mahasabha, later became High Commissioner to Ceylon.[4]

Golwalkar did not include Gandhi's name among the very many illustrious names he listed in 1939 on page 42 of his book *We or our Nationhood Defined*. His *Bunch of Thoughts* (1966) excoriated Gandhi at several places unmistakably without mentioning him by name, especially in Chapter X on 'Territorial Nationalism' as distinct from 'Cultural Nationalism' (by which the RSS and the BJP swear even now).

After denouncing Communists, Golwalkar turned to the Congress. 'The other movement led by Congress has had more disastrous and degrading effects on the country. Most of the tragedies and evils that have overtaken our country during the last few decades and are even today corroding our national life are its direct outcome' (1968 edition, p. 145,). He added in an insidious passage (page 153): 'Here we had leaders who were, as if, pledged to sap all manliness from their own people.' It was 'a self-destructive leadership.'

Soon after independence, Gandhi interacted with the RSS and its supremo, Golwalkar. He had received complaints about its activities from Asaf Ali, president of the Delhi PCC in 1942 (*CWMG* 76: 401). RSS men obstructed his prayer meeting on April 3, 1947. Gandhi called it 'a big organization.' A letter came from the RSS disowning them (*CWMG* 87: 195, 202).

Gandhi met Golwalkar in September 1947. He told an RSS rally on September 16 that he had mentioned to Golwalkar

the various complaints about the Sangh that he had received in Calcutta and Delhi. The Guruji had assured him that though he would not vouch for the correct behaviour of every member of the Sangh, the policy of the Sangh was purely service of the Hindus and Hinduism and that too not at the cost of anyone else. The Sangh did not believe in aggression. It did not believe in ahimsa. It taught the art of self-defence. It never taught retaliation. (*CWMG* 89: 193)

Earlier on September 12, Gandhi told his prayer meeting that he 'had been told that the hands of this organization too were steeped in blood. The Guruji assured him that this was untrue. . . . It stood for peace and he had asked Gandhiji to make his "Golwalkar views public"' (*CWMG* 89: 177).

Gandhi, obviously, was not assured, for he told the All India Congress Committee (AICC) two months later, on November 15: 'I have heard it said that Sangh is at the root of all this mischief. . . . Hinduism cannot be saved by orgies of murder' (*CWMG* 90: 43). The next day (November 16) he spoke of 'the Hindu Mahasabha assisted by members of the RSS who wish that all Muslims should be driven away from the Indian Union' (*CWMG* 90: 50). He had received complaints about their behaviour in Rajkot also. 'Is it true that they have harassed the Muslims? If not, who has?' (*CWMG* 90: 143)

Gandhi went on a fast from January 13. The RSS was among the signatories to the declaration embodying assurances to Muslims that persuaded Gandhi to break his fast on January 18 (*CWMG* 90: 444). Still, Gandhi was none too assured. It would be a breach of faith if they break the assurances 'in other places. I have been observing that this sort of deception is being practised in the country these days on a large scale' (*CWMG* 90: 445).

This cold point of the record must be read with the testimonies of two close associates, Jawaharlal Nehru and Pyarelal. Nehru wrote to Sardar Patel on October 27, 1948:

> I remember Bapu telling me after his first meeting with Golwalkar that he was partly impressed by him *but at the same time did not trust him*. After his second or third meeting he expressed a very strong opinion against Golwalkar and the RSS *and said that it was impossible to rely upon their word*. They appear to be highly reasonable when talked to but they had no compunction in acting in exact contradiction to what they said. My own impression has been the same.

Pyarelal's account is fairly detailed. His comments are pertinent.

He was the Mahatma's devoted Boswell and privy to his confidence: 'It was common knowledge that the RSS . . . had been behind the bulk of the killings in the city [Delhi] as also in various other parts of India' (p. 439). He records: 'A member of Gandhiji's party interjected that the RSS people had done a fine job of work at Wah refugee camp. They had shown discipline, courage and capacity for hard work. "But don't forget," answered Gandhiji, "even so had Hitler's Nazis and the Fascists under Mussolini."' He characterized the RSS as a 'communal body with a totalitarian outlook.'[5]

On January 20, two days after Gandhi broke his fast, one Madanlal Pahwa threw a bomb which exploded some 20 metres away from where Gandhi was sitting. Someone said it was the prank of an irresponsible young man. Pyarelal writes: 'Gandhiji laughed and exclaimed, "The fool: Don't you see, there is a terrible and widespread conspiracy behind it?"'[6] Ten days later, that conspiracy accomplished its objective. Gandhi was assassinated by Nathuram Godse in conspiracy with others. Pyarelal's record of what became known later is very relevant today and bears quotation *in extenso*:

> A letter which Sardar Patel received after the assassination from a young man, who according to his own statement had been gulled into joining the RSS organization but was later disillusioned, described how members of the RSS at some places had been instructed beforehand to tune in their radio sets on the fateful Friday for the 'good news'. After the news, sweets were distributed in RSS circles at several places including Delhi. When the RSS was later banned by an order of the Government, the local police chief in one of the Indian States, according to the Sardar's correspondent, sent word to the organizers to close their office 'for thirteen days' as a sign of mourning, and disperse but not to disband. The rot was so insidious and widespread that only the supreme sacrifice could arrest or remove it.

That rot has now reappeared and is desperate to quell its stench by dousing itself with the scent that surrounds the name of Gandhi – a man against whom, as Pyarelal recalled, they had waged 'a sustained campaign of calumny . . . for over a quarter of a century.'

5

RSS Front Organizations: The BJP–VHP–BD Trident

The RSS was established in Nagpur in September 1925, on Dussehra day. On October 21, 1951, it floated a political party, the Bharatiya Jan Sangh, with an eye on the first general election in 1952. The BJS dissolved itself on May 1, 1977 in order to merge with the Janata Party. On April 5, 1980 it was revived as the Bharatiya Janata Party.

Meanwhile, Golwalkar had set up the Vishwa Hindu Parishad (VHP) in Mumbai on August 29, 1964. The VHP set up the Bajrang Dal in May–June 1984. The timing was significant – the VHP had passed a resolution in April 1984 for the 'liberation' of the site on which stood the Babri Masjid at Ayodhya.

RSS men have been put in charge of all the three organizations, the BJP, the VHP and the Bajrang Dal – Advani, Vajpayee, Murli Manohar Joshi of the BJP, Ashok Singhal of the VHP, and Vinay Katiyar, erstwhile organization secretary of the ABVP, the *parivar's* student front, of the Bajrang Dal. This trident of front organizations has led the RSS assault on Indian polity and society.

THE BIRTH OF BJP

The Bharatiya Janata Party (BJP) has come a long way since it was founded in 1980. That the BJP won but two seats in the Lok Sabha elections in 1984 and 88 in 1989 is impressive in itself despite the fact that both the results need qualification. The 1984 debacle was due to the pro-Rajiv wave in the wake of Indira Gandhi's assassination. The steep rise in fortunes in 1989 was due to, as Advani has repeatedly boasted, to the BJP's resolution on Ayodhya adopted on the eve of the elections at Palampur on June 11, 1989. What is clear is that it has carved out for itself a significant constituency in the country. Today, it leads the government at the centre, and runs governments in several states. It has found for itself many allies all over the country, including important constituents of the erstwhile United Front like the Telugu Desam and the DMK. It is beginning to register a presence, electoral and otherwise, in the south and the north-east, areas where traditionally it has been weak.

It is instructive today to look at what Advani had said when the BJP was formed. In an interview to the RSS weekly *Panchjanya* (Deepavali 1980), Advani disagreed with the view that the Janata Party would die because it had no ideology:

> *Advani*: No. I do not agree with it for in India a party based on ideology can at the most come to power in a small area. It cannot win the confidence of *the entire country* – neither the Communist Party nor the Jan Sangh in its original form.
>
> *Panchjanya*: But by ignoring the ideological appeal will you be able to keep together the cadres on the basis of these ideals?
>
> *Advani*: Effort is being made to make them understand. That is why I want the debate to go on. In this context, some people have criticized me although even during the Jan Sangh days I used to advocate these ideas. I have already said that the Jan Sangh was initially built as a party based on ideology but slowly it departed from that course.
>
> *Panchjanya*: However, despite its ideological anchorage, the Jan Sangh's appeal was steadily increasing.
>
> *Advani*: The appeal increased to the extent the ideology got diluted. Wherever the ideology was strong, its appeal diminished.

Contrast this with what he said on the eve of the Somnath–Ayodhya *rath yatra*: 'Ideologically, I am ranged against all political parties because of this issue. All political parties think alike.' The issue was clearly defined. It was not the Ram Janmabhoomi issue. It was a 'crusade in defence of *Hindutva* and a crusade against pseudo-secularism.' Its goal is to break from the Nehru–Gandhi ethos and recast the polity.

Time was when the BJP tried to distance itself from those who spoke a language of such stridency. Vajpayee said in an interview in August 1980 that the BJP was different from the BJS 'in many ways': 'Having tasted power once, we realized that unless we became a party of the national mainstream and enjoyed support from all sections, we could not become a national alternative.'

Yet, this quest to become a party of the national mainstream has not entailed a break from the RSS. Far from it. The BJP was born as a result of the split in the Janata Party on the issue of some of its members' membership of the RSS, a fact which BJP leaders never cease to emphasize. But while in 1980 they claimed to be the real heirs to the Janata Party of Jayaprakash Narayan rather than to the Jan Sangh, today they claim to be closer to the RSS than the Jan Sangh was. Speaking to an RSS gathering in Coimbatore in 1990, Advani said: 'While in the case of the BJS the linkage [with the RSS] was only ideological, in the case of the BJP the linkage is both ideological and historical.' He asked his audience to realize that 'the BJP which you described as a good party is good only because of its association with the RSS' (*TT* May 17).

Therefore, it seems amazing today that on February 26, 1980, Advani himself wrote to the Janata Party's president, Chandra Shekhar: 'Our commitment to the party's principles and programmes, the concepts of Gandhian socialism and secularism, has been total and unequivocal.' This, of course, was to secularism as understood by the Janata Party – something which Advani subsequently dubbed as pseudo-secularism. What has changed in so short a time?

ABANDONING JANATA PARTY FOR RSS

As events unfolded, the new party did not act as if it was heir to the Janata at all. On August 31, 1980, Vajpayee, then BJP president, defended the RSS and accused the Government of appeasing the minorities. At the party's first plenary convention in Bombay on December 28, 1980, Vajpayee significantly recalled the history of the Jan Sangh and its sessions in Bombay. 'Gandhian socialism' was affirmed as one of the five commitments. The others were nationalism and national integration, democracy, 'positive secularism' and value-based politics. 'Plurality of religious faiths, ideologies, languages' and so on were acknowledged. But not 'composite culture'. There was a dark hint about people with 'extra-territorial loyalties'. A suggestion by Mehboob Ali, a former Janata minister from Rajasthan, that the minorities' interests be protected was brusquely rejected.

Shortly thereafter occurred one of those events whose impact was perceived fully only later – the conversion of a large number of Harijans to Islam at Meenakshipuram in Tamil Nadu in February 1981. RSS chief Balasaheb Deoras said this had brought about an 'awakening' among Hindus. The causes behind this event were purely local in origin. But the event affected the communal atmosphere in the country greatly. The social tensions in Meenakshipuram subsided, but the atmosphere in the country continued to deteriorate. Communal riots took place in several parts of the country, the ones at Moradabad and Meerut being the worst.

The deterioration was due to a large degree to Indira Gandhi's changed style of politics. Not only was there a withdrawal from a populist to a managerial style of conducting national affairs, but inherent in this was also a turnabout from secular to communal politics. She had forged a new winning coalition in the Hindi homeland. The minorities had begun to move away from the Congress (I). Indira Gandhi made a bid for the Hindu vote, to the BJP's discomfiture.

The crunch came in the elections to the Delhi Metropolitan Council in February 1983 and to the Jammu and Kashmir Assembly in June. The BJP fared miserably in both its strongholds. It won 19 seats as against the Congress (I)'s 34 in the 56-member Metropolitan Council. It could not win a single Assembly seat from Jammu and polled only 8.15 per cent vote. The results shook the BJP. In 1983 it formed the National Democratic Alliance with Charan Singh's Lok Dal to work together in the legislatures as a joint bloc and 'to coordinate their activities outside as well as in elections.' It was ready to form a National Democratic Front with others.

The BJP found the ground being gradually cut under its feet. 'Indira Gandhi's standing as a true leader of the Hindu community has now received electoral imprimatur,' remarked Nikhil Chakravarty, senior journalist. When Vajpayee participated in the VHP's Ekatmata Yagna along with Advani and paid tributes to 'the organizing skill of the RSS, the backbone of the Parishad' in November 1983, he was discomfited to find the VHP's president singing praises of Indira Gandhi. When the BJP's National Council ended its deliberations in Indore on January 8, 1984, Vajpayee could not conceal his dissatisfaction with the party's progress. It could no longer hope to be the national alternative and acknowledged that now 'no single party can'. There were strains in the relations with Charan Singh. Vajpayee tried to reach out to the RSS by calling it an inherent part of the BJP's structure and extolling the unbreakable relationship. But Balasaheb Deoras was intent on placating Indira Gandhi (*TH* January 30, 1984), and Rajendra Singh, RSS General Secretary, admitted: 'We have supported the Government on national issues' (March 24, 1984).

It was a cruel dilemma for the BJP. Neither the RSS line nor unity with opposition parties held any promise. Vajpayee told James M. Markham of *The New York Times* (June 14, 1984) shortly after Operation Bluestar, 'Mrs Gandhi is playing a very dangerous game. The long-term interests of the country are being sacrificed to short-term gains. But encouraging Hindu chauvinism is not going to pay. As the majority community, Hindus must be above parochial politics. . . . She wanted to take advantage of the Hindu backlash.' These sage words could justly be applied to Advani's *rath yatra* later. But between then and Vajpayee's last-ditch stand in 1984 lay a period which saw a series of compromises by this pathetically tragic figure in Indian politics.

Indira Gandhi's assassination threw the entire Opposition off balance. It was too demoralized even to promise to work together if elected to power. Rajiv Gandhi swept the elections, riding on the sympathy wave.

When the BJPs National Executive met in Calcutta in March 1985, Vajpayee proposed that a working group be set up to reflect on the course the party had adopted and suggest a way out of the morass in which it found itself. Was the BJPs defeat due to 'our decision to merge the Jan Sangh with the Janata Party in 1977 and withdraw from it an 1980?' 'Should the BJP go back and revive the Bharatiya Jan Sangh?' That in his view 'will amount to a slide back.' The BJP had 'no truck with the VHP' he stressed.

The RSS, however, was ready with its answer to the BJP's dilemma: *Organizer*, in an editorial on April 7 titled 'Revamping the BJP', opined that the remedy lay in the restoration of the leadership's rapport with a sizable section of its selfless cadres (i.e., the RSS) still alienated since the Janata days. The BJP's stance of positive secularism and Gandhian socialism, it argued, had alienated the party. What mattered was ideological cohesion.

Predictably, the working group's 47-page report, while not indicting the leadership, recommended that the concept enunciated by Jan Sangh leader Deen Dayal Upadhyaya, 'integral humanism' be adopted as 'the basic philosophy' of the BJP instead of 'Gandhian socialism', though the Gandhian approach to socio-economic system' could be adopted as one of the commitments. Vajpayee denied that there was any crisis of identity. Asked if it meant a return to the Jan Sangh, he countered: 'when did we get away from Jan Sangh?' On November 6, 1977, however, he had said exactly the opposite: 'When we joined the Janata Party, we had given up our old beliefs and faiths and there was no question of going back.' No less revealing was his remark, on July 22, 1985, that 'we wanted to assert our views in the [Janata] Government but the Government broke up too soon. Had we been in power for some more time we would have imparted a new thinking to India's politics.'

ASCENDANT RSS

Two events then took place later which provided considerable grist to the BJP's mill. On January 31, 1986, Faizabad District Judge K.M. Pandey ordered that the locks on the gates of the premises of the Babri Masjid be opened. On February 25 the Muslim Women's Bill was moved in Parliament to override the Supreme Court's ruling in the Shah Bano case. It was in this atmosphere that the BJP held its second plenary session in New Delhi on May 9, 1986, with Advani replacing Vajpayee as president.

Advani flatly denied that the BJP was hardening its stand and attributed the changes to the altered situation. By then Rajiv Gandhi's popularity had begun to wane. The Bofors disclosures in April 1987 accelerated the process and the Opposition's fortunes revived. The BJP had its share of the gains when it formed a coalition with Devi Lal's Lok Dal after his spectacular victory in the Haryana Assembly elections in June 1987.

But there was no doubt that the RSS was now in the ascendant. In October 1987 it organized a meeting of prominent swayamsevaks working in the BJP, the VHP, the ABVP and the BMS, which was attended by Vajpayee and Advani. On October 21, Advani justified the conclave. 'After all there is a linkage, all these organizations consist of people belonging to the RSS.' On November 16, Deoras said the RSS entry into politics 'in the near future' was not ruled out.

There began in 1988 a clear hardening of the BJP's line. This was, however, by no means sudden, but had been in the making for some time. Two features of this phase stand out. One is candour. More than ever before were a series of blatantly communal utterances by Advani. The other is an openness about the linkage with the RSS coupled with greater assertion by the latter. The BJP shed its ambiguities and the RSS stopped its pro-Congress (I) statements. Merrily or sadly, Vajpayee sailed with these currents.

The BJP's plenary session in Agra on April 8, 1988 was a landmark. And Advani, who had on April 4, 1980, 'unconditionally' pledged himself 'to preserving the composite culture' of India, now discovered that 'emphasis on the composite character of Indian culture is generally an attempt to disown its essentially Hindu spirit and content.' At an RSS meeting in Coimbatore he said India's culture 'is essentially a Hindu culture' and it 'should be reflected in the various policies, programmes, attitudes and positions we take.'

The BJP now openly began vowing that it sought to protect Hindu interests. On September 30, 1990, in Mumbai, Advani complained that today's leaders were afraid of speaking for Hindus. In the same breath he asked the minorities to accept this country and its culture. A day earlier, in Ahmedabad, Advani said that even after forty years of Independence almost all political parties which have ruled the country have done nothing for the 'betterment of the Hindu community' but had taken 'special interest' in 'appeasing' the minorities for their own 'political gains'. The next day in Bombay he went further: 'When Muslims, Sikhs and other communities practice their religion, then we call them secular, but if parties like the BJP and the Shiv Sena practice Hinduism, then we are branded as communal.' The semantic sleight of hand in juxtaposing a people's 'practice' of religion with that of a party apart, the line is a dangerous one to pursue in a plural society.

The Jan Morcha and later the Janata Dal could not possibly have an alliance with the BJP, especially in its (the BJP's) post-1986 incarnation. It was invited to the Suraj Kund opposition conclave by

Devi Lal but was shunned thereafter. The BJP both resented this isolation as well as prided itself on it. Its support to the National Front government, spelt out in Advani's letter of November 29, 1989, was with specified 'reservations' – Article 370, uniform Civil Code, Human Rights Commission and Ram Janmabhoomi.

The Janata Dal government's stand on the Mandal report widened the differences. For obvious reasons, the BJP perceived it as a threat to its strategy to unify the Hindu community on the plank of Hindutva. Asked how long the BJP's support would continue, Vajpayee ominously said on September 25: 'We are waiting for the right time.'

But it was the RSS which called the shots. Towards the end of August a meeting of the RSS top brass in New Delhi decided to adopt a tough line on the Ayodhya issue even at the risk of rupturing ties with the government. On September 12 came Advani's announcement of the *rath yatra* from Somnath to Ayodhya. The speeches he made subsequently were defiant and communal. The issue, he said, was not the construction of the temple but the 'basis of nationalism in the country.' He was out to restore 'national pride,' echoed Vajpayee on September 23, while Advani amplified that the feeling of nationalism would glow. It is a 'crusade in defence of Hindutva,' he thundered on September 24. The next day he called it 'the second phase of nationalist renaissance after Independence.' In November 1989, he claimed: 'if the BJP had not tried to channel the feelings of Hinuds, the consequences for national unity would not have been good.' The subsequent record shows these words were more a threat, rather than an assurance.

1989 AND AFTER

The 1989 general election yielded a fragmented verdict. The Left Parties as well as the BJP pledged support to the National Front, headed by the Janata Dal, from outside in order to enable its leader, Vishwanath Pratap Singh, to form a government. However, Advani's letter to V.P. Singh and N.T. Rama Rao, as Convenor of the National Front, dated November 29, 1989, contained this stipulation:

> If it is acknowledged by the JD that though the JD and BJP differ on issues like Article 370, Uniform Civil Code, Human Rights Commission, Rama Janmabhoomi, etc., the JD does not regard the BJP as communal,

Jana Sangh/BJP performance in Lok Sabha elections, 1952–1999

	Seats won	Percentage of votes
1952	3	3.1
1957	4	5.9
1962	14	6.4
1967	35	9.4
1971	22	7.4
1977	91	14.0
1980	15	8.6
1984	2	7.4
1989	85	11.4
1991	120	20.1
1996	161	21.34
1998	180	25.6
1999	182	23.7

Note 1952–71: Bharatiya Jana Sangh; 1977–80: Jana Sangh faction in Janata Party; 1984–99: Bharatiya Janata Party.

that would go a long way in removing misgivings in our rank and file. I hope the NF will take note of these reservations and exert to remove them. . . . Even while expressing these reservations, *we have not made our support to you conditional to your agreeing to remove them.* In response to your letter, the BJP wishes to convey to you its readiness to give general but critical support to the NF Government. (*TH* November 30, 1989).

Advani went back on this only a few months later when he launched the *rath yatra* which could not have failed to bring down the National Front government. The reference to the Human Rights Commission was a veiled demand for the abolition of the Minorities Commission. The BJP leaders were privy to the Janata Party Government's decision to set up the Commission in 1979. The RSS demanded its abolition and replacement by an HRC. The BJP fell in line.

On February 27, 1990, elections were held to assemblies of eight states. The BJP won the largest number, 498 seats, against the Dal's 458 and the Congress (I)'s 444. It formed governments in Madhya Pradesh, Rajasthan and Himachal Pradesh. On August 7, 1990 Prime Minister V.P. Singh announced his government's decision to implement the Mandal Report which had recommended that 27 per cent of government jobs be reserved for backward castes. Advani's riposte was sharp and calculated. He declared, on September 12, that he would go on a *rath yatra* from Somnath to Ayodhya from September

25 to October 30. The challenge to the National Front Government could not have been more explicit.

Following Advani's arrest in Bihar, by Laloo Prasad Yadav's government, the BJP withdrew its support from V.P. Singh's government on October 23. It was voted out of office on a no-confidence motion on November 7 by 356 votes against 151 with 6 abstentions. Both the BJP and the Congress (I) voted for the motion. Chandra Shekhar split the Janata Dal on November 5 and formed a government with Congress (I) support. It was, predictably, withdrawn in March 1991. The Lok Sabha was dissolved. On Rajiv Gandhi's tragic assassination in May, P.V. Narasimha Rao became leader of the Congress (I) Parliamentary Party and was sworn in as Prime Minister on June 21.

'Fantastic' was Advani's description of Rao's minority government as it wended its way trying to please only to overreached itself. The Union Home Secretary Madhav Godbole's memoirs, *Unfinished Innings*, contain a detailed record of the parleys with the Sangh *parivar* and the government's connivance at the moves by the RSS, BJP, VHP, Bajrang Dal and the Shiv Sena to demolish the Babri mosque.

The Sangh *parivar* accomplished its objective a mere year and half after Rao became Prime Minister.

It inscribed its name indelibly in the annals of infamy on December 6, 1992 in perpetration of a crime that ranks only with Gandhi's assassination on January 30, 1948. The RSS was banned after both the crimes.

THE RSS FRONT ORGANIZATIONS

The Sangh *parivar* is playing a monstrous fraud on the Indian electorate generally and on minorities in particular. Its attempts to suggest that the BJP differs from the VHP are as dishonest as they are desperate. Everyone knows that the two are partners in a common enterprise run by their parent, the RSS. 'I am Atal Behari Vajpayee and I am different from Mr Ashok Singhal, Working President of the VHP. Ask the VHP about its stand on Kashi and Mathura. Our stand is clear. Kashi and Mathura are not on our agenda. Full stop', Vajpayee said in Lucknow on December 30, 1997. He added: 'Everyone knows that the VHP and the BJP are different organizations.' In that very city only the day before, Singhal had said, 'It is time to catch Muslims

This bit came out in the evidence before the Citizens' Commission too.

Clearly, there is a case to answer and not for the accused alone. Kuldip Nayyar reported in *The Statesman* of February 24, 1993 that the RSS boss, Balasaheb Deoras, 'at Nagpur received the call himself. It was as if he was anxiously awaiting something important. The two Marathi words communicated were: *Fateh zali* (work completed). He is said to have felt relieved.' *The Hindu's* correspondent reported (November 2, 1992) that the VHP's 'confrontationist path on the Ayodhya issue was the direct outcome of the hardline stance adopted by the RSS at its recent Ujjain conclave.' That conclave ended on October 27, 1992. The rest is history.

UNION HOME MINSTER AS AN ACCUSED

A minister in government who provides moral help to militants up in arms against the state is a certifiable security risk. If he happens to be Home Minister in charge of national security as well, he deserves the boot from the President. Advani faces a charge-sheet prepared by the Central Bureau of Investigation (CBI), which is now under his control. Dated October 5, 1993, it alleges, after a thorough investigation, that he participated in a conspiracy to demolish the masjid on December 6, 1992 and committed grave offences in pursuance of that conspiracy. It also charged two other ministers, Murli Manohar Joshi and Uma Bharati.

On February 4, 1994, the Supreme Court issued notice for contempt of court against Advani and others. On August 27, 1994, Special Judicial Magistrate Mahipal Sirohi found that a *prima facie* case existed which warranted committal of those accused by the CBI to trial by a Sessions Court which alone could pass sentence in a grave case like this. On September 9, 1997, Jagdish Prasad Srivastava, Additional Sessions Judge (Ayodhya Episode), Lucknow, 'concluded that in the present case a criminal conspiracy to demolish the disputed structure of Ram Janam Bhoomi/Babri Masjid was hatched by the accused persons in the beginning of 1990 and was completed on 6.12.1992. Shri Lal Krishan Advani and others hatched criminal conspiracies to demolish the disputed premises on different times at different places. Therefore, I find a *prima facie* case to charge Shri Bala Saheb Thakre, Shri Lal Krishan Advani, Shri Kalyan

Singh, Shri Vinay Katiyar' and others under Section 147, 153(A), 153(B), 259, 295(A) and 505 read with Section 120(B) of the Indian Penal Code.

Thus, the case was found proved *prima facie* warranting a regular trial. *Matters had gone far beyond a charge-sheet filed in a court by the police.* Two judicial officers, the committing Magistrate and the Sessions Judge, found that a *prima facie* case was established on the facts.

However, one formality remained for the trial to begin. Section 228 (2) of the Criminal Procedure Code lays down that where the Sessions Judge 'frames any charge,' as in the Ayodhya case, 'the charge shall be read and explained to the accused, and the accused shall be asked whether he pleads guilty of the offence charge or claims to be tried.' In short, the accused must himself be *physically present* in order that his or her plea to the charge is recorded. The lawyer's presence will not suffice.

Accordingly Judge Srivastava ordered: 'All the accused persons are directed to be presented in the Court on 17-10-1997 for framing of the charges.' By filing revision applications in the Allahabad High Court and absenting themselves, the accused have averted the opening of the trial for a full two years since October 17, 1997.

The Sessions Judge's 61-page order is a public document which has been published in full as a CPI(M) publication entitled 'Ayodhya Conspiracy of Saffron Brigade Unmasked'. The Sessions Judge's order recorded: 'On 5-12-1992 a *secret* meeting was held at the house of Sh. Vinay Katiyar which was *attended by Sh. Lal Krishan Advani*, Pawan Kumar Pandey *and a final decision to demolish disputed structure was taken.* Their argument was that there was a ban on construction not on demolition and accused No. 1 to 38 assembled near Ram Janam Bhoomi/Babri Masjid on 6-12-92 and *Sh. Lal Krishan Advani categorically said in his public speech before the demolition of disputed structure that "Today is the last day of Kar Seva. Kar Sewaks would perform last Kar Seva."* When he came to know that central force was proceeding from Faizabad to Ayodhya then he [*Advani*] *asked the public to block National Highway so that central forces do not reach Ram Janambhoomi.* Prosecution has also contended that when disputed structure was being pulled down *Sh. Advani asked Kalyan Singh not to tender his resignation till the disputed structure is completely pulled down'.*

What was Advani's defence? 'No masjid existed on the spot, as no Namaz was ever held there. Disputed structure was a mandir *for centuries*. The court had restrained from constructing mandir. There was no injunction against demolition of the mandir.'

And the Sessions Judge's finding? 'On a careful perusal of evidence produced by the prosecution in the present case, I have come to conclusion that the *prima facie* evidence as alleged against the accused persons is made out.'

In paragraph 36, he traced Advani's movement just prior to the offence and concluded (para 37) that he was very much a party to the conspiracy. In a later interview (*Outlook*, December 20, 1999), Advani said: 'I had nothing to do with the demolition.' The Judge's Order, however, recorded, 'As per Ms. Ruchira Gupta, PW-145 that Shri Advani declared that CRPF may arrive at any time. Therefore, all the people should raise barricade on the main roads so as to prevent CRPF from coming near the spot.' This was also reported by the correspondents of *The Hindu* and *Indian Express* (December 7, 1992).

Advani says that the demolition of the Babri Masjid was a 'political offence'. What will he say to the militants who indulge in acts of violence in, say, Kashmir or the North-East? 'As for the demand for my resignation,' says Advani, 'there is a clear distinction between a political case and being charge-sheeted in any other case, however motivated it may have been.' The hawala case, over which he resigned from the Lok Sabha on being charge-sheeted, 'involved moral turpitude of sorts, relating to corruption'. The implication is plain – the demolition of a house of worship does not involve 'moral turpitude'. Prime Minster Vajpayee sang the same tune on December 7, 1999. 'There is no corruption charge against them, nor any allegation of misuse of office. You know there is a difference between charges of corruption and this kind of case.' Can the demolition of a house of worship be characterized as a 'political offence' at all as the expression is understood in the civilized world?

By all established definitions of 'terrorism', the demolition of the Babri mosque was a 'terrorist act'. By all established definitions of a 'political offence', terrorism falls far outside it. Were Advani's and Vajpayee's test to pass muster, the armed militants in Kashmir and in northeastern India, the People's War Group (PWG) and other naxalite groups would be beyond the reach of the law. It is disgraceful that in order to save Advani's tarnished skin, he and the Prime Minister should dishonestly stretch the law and set a dangerous precedent for use by law-breakers in power in the future and armed militants on the rampage at present.

To both of them, as well as the other charge-sheeted ministers, one would pose a simple question: what about the assassins of Gandhi, led by the RSS's own Nathuram Godse, and those of Indira Gandhi and Rajiv Gandhi? Were they also political offenders like L.K. Advani, Murli Manohar Joshi and Uma Bharati?

THE DAY AFTER

The Narasimha Rao Government lost no time in shutting the stable doors after it had allowed the communal beast to flee. On December 10, 1992, notifications were issued under the Unlawful Activities (Prevention) Act, 1967 banning the RSS, the VHP, the Bajrang Dal, and, in a show of balance, the Jamaat-e-Islami and the Islamic Sewak Sangh. On June 4, 1993 Justice P.K. Bahri of the Delhi High Court, sitting on the Tribunal appointed under the Act, upheld the ban on the VHP but quashed the ones against the RSS and the Bajrang Dal. He however, spoke of 'the laudable objects being pursued by VHP.' If the Government sought consciously to have its cosmetic ban on the RSS quashed by a judge whose 'public philosophy' was manifestly sympathetic to these bodies, it could not have prepared the case for the bans with greater ineptitude. (See the writer's critiques in *Frontline*, July 2 and September 10, 1993.) The Government's counsel rightly said 'the BJP is a political wing of the RSS.'

The evidence on this linkage before the Tribunal itself was overwhelming. If RSS supremo Balasaheb Deoras was a trustee of the VHP, Singhal of the VHP was a member of the RSS. A VHP publication *Virat Hindu Sammelan* refers to the RSS's activities and those of the 'sister' organizations. Singhal attended most meetings of the RSS's executive bodies from 1989 to 1992. The VHP admitted to the Tribunal that the RSS 'is a kind of university' which produces 'great nationalists.' RSS leader Rajendra Singh used other metaphors: 'training institute' and 'a father's house.' Acharya Giriraj Kishore of the VHP told the Tribunal that his press release of December 2 'had mentioned that the kar sevaks would be functioning [on December 6] within the discipline to be enforced by RSS workers.' Formally, both the RSS and the VHP asserted that they were 'not inter-related' or 'inter-linked.' The RSS has in its reply denied the contents of the speeches imputed to the leaders of the VHP and the Bajrang Dal and in some cases tried to justify them.

Rajendra Singh excelled himself: 'He deposed that he had little knowledge of the working of VHP and Bajrang Dal and whatever knowledge he has is derived from news reports.' But the RSS reply cited facts pertaining to the VHP and the Bajrang Dal 'based on personal knowledge of this witness' and 'prepared on his instructions alone.' A book brought on the record by the RSS itself, *RSS: A Vision in Action*, referred to the Sangh *parivar* and the VHP as its members.

Why then did the Tribunal completely ignore the evidence on this point? Justice Bahri's own outlook is anything but enlightened: 'The laudable objects being pursued by VHP cannot be objected, for strengthening the various Hindu sects for uniting them' (p. 284). He proceeded to refer to invasions by Muslim rulers, conversions to Islam (p. 284) and to British policies 'so that those Muslims should not get assimilated in the mainstream of the culture of this country' (p. 285). This is the very view which the Sangh *parivar* espouses.

President's rule was imposed on December 15, 1992 in three BJP-ruled States – Rajasthan, Madhya Pradesh and Himachal Pradesh. The Chief Minister of Uttar Pradesh Kalyan Singh had invited this action by resigning on December 6. The Supreme Court upheld the three contested Proclamations under Article 356 of the Constitution on March 11, 1994 in S.R. Bommai vs. Union of India & Ors. ([1994] 3 Supreme Court Cases page 1). Seven of the nine judges who decided the case held that secularism is part of the unamendable 'basic structure' of the Constitution. Justices P.B. Sawant and Kuldip Singh cited the BJP's 1991 Election Manifesto among the 'professions and acts which are evidently against the Constitution.'

Particularly noteworthy were Justice P.B. Jeevan Reddy's observations:

Shri Parasaran is right in his submission that what happened on December 6, 1992 was no ordinary event, *that it was the outcome of a sustained campaign carried out over a number of years throughout the country and that it was the result of the speeches, acts and deeds of several leaders of BJP and other organizations.* The event had serious repercussions not only within the country but outside as well. It put in doubt the very secular credentials of this nation and its Government – and those credentials had to be redeemed. The situation had many dimensions, social, religious, political and international. Rarely do such occasions arise in the life of a nation. The situation was an extraordinary one, its repercussions could not be foretold at that time. Nobody could say with definiteness what would happen and where? The situation was not only unpredictable, it was a fast-evolving one. The communal situation was tense. It could explode anywhere at any time. On the material placed before us, including the reports of the Governors, we cannot say that the President had no relevant material before him on the basis of which he could form the satisfaction that the BJP Governments of Madhya Pradesh, Rajasthan and Himachal Pradesh cannot dissociate themselves from the action and its consequences and that these Governments, controlled by one and the same party, whose leading lights were actively campaigning for the demolition of the disputed structure, cannot be dissociated from the acts and deeds of the leaders of BJP. In the then prevailing situation, the Union of India thought it necessary to ban certain organizations including RSS and here were Governments which were headed by persons who 'swore by the values and traditions of the RSS' and were giving 'overt and covert support to the associate communal organization' (vide report of the Governor of Madhya Pradesh). The Governor of Himachal Pradesh reported that 'the Chief Minister himself is a member of RSS'. The Governor of Rajasthan reported that the ban on RSS and other organizations was not being implemented because of the intimate connection between the members of the Government and those organizations. The three Governors also spoke of the part played by the members of the Government in sending and welcoming back the kar sevaks. They also expressed the opinion that these Governments cannot be expected, in the circumstances, to function objectively and impartially in dealing with the emerging law and order situation, which had all the ominous makings of a communal conflagration.

In 2000 AD, however, as Chairman of the Law Commission, Justice Jeevan Reddy forgot these well chosen words when he opined that 'religious militancy . . . had first raised its head in 1993 with bomb explosions in Mumbai' not on December 6, 1992, to go no further.

In the elections to the assemblies of those states in November 1993, the BJP lost power in Uttar Pradesh, Madhya Pradesh and Himachal Pradesh but returned to power in Rajasthan (95 seats in a House of 200).

The hawala scandal which was out in the open in January 1996 dealt a severe blow to Advani's prestige. Like the others mentioned in 'the Jain diaries', he was discharged by the court. But the damage was done. Arun Jaitley, made the perfect comment on the case on September 16, 1998 during *The Statesman's* annual debate: 'The accused in the Jain Hawala Case were let off not by the judiciary but by the investigative agencies which did not do a good job' (*TS* September 17, 1998).

At the Mumbai session of the BJP's National Executive in November 1995 Advani had accepted the obvious – his lack of credibility – and declared magnanimously that Vajpayee would be the next Prime Minister. After the 1996 General Election, to everyone's dismay, President Shankar Dayal Sharma appointed Vajpayee as Prime Minister, on May 15, despite his lack of majority in the House.[2] Vajpayee resigned on May 28 when faced with certain defeat on the motion of confidence. In sheer desperation, he offered that day to 'freeze' the three contentious issues (the Ram temple, uniform civil code, Article 370) but found that it had no takers. He offered an accord 'on the basis of a consensus and a common minimum programme'. But, in vain. The 13 day wonder did the BJP little good.

Significantly, during the election campaign, its spokesperson, Sushma Swaraj, had categorically declared on January 2, 1998: 'There will be no CMP [Common Minimum Programme] before elections'. The National Democratic Alliance was forged in 1998, of sheer necessity and with ill-concealed reservations. On September 12, 1998, shortly after he had endorsed the National Agenda for Governance on March 18, Advani told party workers in New Delhi: 'We have taken up those components that are acceptable to all the allies. We will wait for the remaining components to be accepted . . . those who taunt us by saying that we have dropped the core issues, introducing a uniform civil code, abrogating Article 370 and Ayodhya, are obviously wrong.' And, this from one who believes that 'for a coalition to function and to endure, then there has to be a dominant partner in the coalition ' (*Sunday*, November 2, 1997).

7

CURRENT AGENDAS

RSS AND CHRISTIANS

On December 4, 1998, nearly 23 million Christians across the country observed a protest day demanding that the governments at the Centre and in the states check the growing violence against members of the community. A letter of protest, drawn up by the United Christians' Forum for Human Rights (UCFHR), said: 'Since January 1998 there has been more violence against the Christian community than in all the 50 years of the country's Independence. Nuns have been raped, priests executed, Bibles burnt, churches demolished, educational institutions destroyed and religious people harassed.' This is *persecution* in the strict dictionary meaning of the word 'pursue with enmity and ill-treatment.' Mabel Rebello of the Congress (I) told the Rajya Sabha that day that '50 per cent of these [incidents] have occurred in Gujarat where the BJP is in power.'

On October 8, Gujarat's Director-General of Police, C.P. Singh, confirmed in an interview to Teesta Setalvad:

> One thing was clear in the pattern of incidents. It was the activists of the Vishwa Hindu Parishad and Bajrang Dal who were taking the law into their own hands, which posed a serious danger to peace in Gujarat. Many of the attacks on the minorities were after these organizations

had whipped up local passions of conversions [by Christian missionaries] and allegedly forced inter-religious marriages . . . our investigations revealed that in most cases these were entirely baseless allegations. (*CC* October 1998)

Two disturbing features of the campaign stand out in bold relief. One is that the attacks mounted steeply after the Bharatiya Janata Party-led Government assumed office in March 1998. The then Archbishop of Delhi, Alan de Lastic, said: 'What I have noticed is that ever since this Government came to power at the Centre, the attacks on Christians and Christian missionaries have increased' (*Sunday*, November 22, 1998). The other is the Government's willful refusal to condemn them. Prime Minister Vajpayee's remarks on December 5 were virtually forced out of him. Union Home Minister L.K. Advani has been false to his oath of office ('do right to all manner of people in accordance with the Constitution and the law without fear or favour, affection or ill-will'). He said in Baroda: 'There is no law and order problem in Gujarat' (*TH* August 3). Three days later the DGP said: 'the VHP and the Bajrang Dal were taking the law into their own hands' (*HT* August 6). He also said that incidents of communal violence had increased manifold over *the last few months*; recently the crime rate in the State had increased by as much as 9.6 per cent. On an average, 39 crimes of serious nature like murder, rape and dacoity were reported in the State every day.' A member of the investigation team sent by the Minorities Commission revealed: 'After initial reluctance, the officials named VHP and Bajrang Dal allegedly involved in the mob attacks on Christians and Muslims' (*IE* August 12). Advani's certificate of good conduct speaks for itself.

Christians did not rush to register their protest, as they did on December 4, but for long kept pleading for succour. On October 1, the national secretary of the All India Catholic Union (AICU), John Dayal, pointedly remarked: 'The AICU is surprised that Union Government and members of the ruling coalition, including the BJP, have not come out categorically in denouncing the violence against Christians.'

The Bajrang Dal threatened Christian-run educational institutions in Karnataka with dire consequences if they did not 'Hinduise' them. Rajendra Singh declared at an RSS camp in Meerut on November 22: 'Muslims and Christians will have to accept Hindu culture as their own if Hindus are to treat them as Indians' (*AA* November 23). The UCFHR bitterly complained in an open letter published on November 19:

> The state has failed to do its duty in protecting the life, dignity and property of the victims. At many places, it seems as if *the Centre* and the State governments have *tacitly supported* the communal groups. How is it otherwise that the State governments have not taken any action against the virulent and anti-national statements of the VHP, RSS, Jagran Manch and Bajrang Dal?

While the Sangh *parivar's* animosity towards Muslims is well-known, its attitude towards Christians took many people by surprise. But, Vishwa Hindu Parishad general secretary Giriraj Kishore said in Chandigarh on November 25: 'Today the Christians constitute a greater threat than the collective threat from separatist Muslim elements.' Describing G.S. Tohra, president of the Shiromani Gurdwara Prabandhak Committee, as a 'separatist', he said, 'all minorities including Muslims and Christian must accept that their ancestors were Hindus.' Ergo, they must all return to the Hindu fold.

Justice P. Venugopal, a former Judge of the Madras High Court, who inquired into Hindu–Christian clashes in Kanyakumari district in March 1982, noted: 'The RSS methodology for provoking communal violence is: (a) rousing communal feelings in the majority community by the propaganda that Christians are not loyal citizens of this country...'

In his fine work Donald Eugene Smith recalled the desecration of a church in Bihar in 1955 and the almost total destruction in 1957 of the Gass Memorial Centre at Raipur.[1]

V.D. Savarkar wrote repeatedly in his book *Hindutva* (1923): '*Hindutva is* different from Hinduism.' For once, he was right. Hinduism is a great religion, it is ancient. Hindutva is an ideology of hate. It is recent. He grouped Muslims and Christians together as ones who do not share 'the tie of the common homage we pay to our great civilization – our Hindu culture.' He added:

> Christian and Mohammedan communities who were but very recently Hindus ... cannot be recognized as Hindus as since their adoption of the new cult they had ceased to own Hindu civilization [*Sanskriti*] as a whole. .... For though Hindusthan to them is Fatherland, as to any other Hindu, yet it is not to them a Holyland too. Their holyland is far

off in Arabia or Palestine.

They are not the only offenders: 'Look at the Jews; neither centuries of prosperity nor sense of gratitude for the shelter they found can make them more attached or even equally attached to the several countries they inhabit.'

Golwalkar's book, *Bunch of Thoughts*, praised the book *Hindutva* and amplified its ideology. The BJP has used it as a political weapon with dangerous consequences. Chapter XII of *Bunch of Thoughts* is devoted to three 'Internal Threats' – Muslims, Christians and the Communists. Of the first two he wrote: 'Together with the change in their faith, gone are the spirit of love and devotion for the nation. Nor does it end there. They have also developed a feeling of identification with the enemies of this land. They look to some foreign lands as their holy places.' They are asked to return to the Hindu fold.

Not that that will be of much help. 'For a Hindu, he gets the first *sanskar* when he is still in his mother's womb. . . . We are, therefore, born as Hindus. About the others, they are born to this world as simple unnamed human beings and later on, either circumcised or baptized, they become Muslims or Christians.' The hatred is unconcealed.

Ram Swarup's tract *Hinduism vis-à-vis Christianity and Islam* contained his views about 'native' faiths. 'What is happening in India is also happening elsewhere. In America even the vestiges of once [*sic*], a rich spiritual culture of the Indians, is no more.' He developed the theme in its sequel *Hindu View of Christianity and Islam* (1992). 'The two ideologies have been active and systematic persecutors of pagan nations, cultures and religions.' He goes on to quote approvingly: 'Gore Vidal says that from a "barbaric Bronze Age text known as Old Testament, three anti-human religions have evolved – Judaism, Christianity and Islam"; he also calls them "sky-god religions".'

Ram Swarup damns all three religions as 'great persecutors'. The Hindu response of old was wrong. He writes:

First, they tried to 'reform' themselves and be like their rulers. . . . One God, a revealed Book and prophets. . . . The Brahmo Samaj, the Arya Samaj, and the Akalis also claimed monotheism and iconoclasm . . . in the case of the Akalis, the new look has also become the basis of a new separatist-militant politics . . .

The second way the Hindus adopted was that of 'synthesis'. The synthesizers claimed that all religions preach the same thing. They found in the Bible and the Quran all the truths of the Upanishads and *vice-versa*.

The wrath wells up as he proceeds and delivers a message *which explains why the country has had to undergo what it has all these years, especially since 1990*:

India became politically free in 1947, but it is ruled by anti-Hindu Hindus. The old mental slavery continues and it has yet to win its cultural and intellectual independence. *India is entering into the second phase of its freedom struggle; the struggle for regaining its Hindu identity.* The new struggle is as difficult as the old one. Hindus are disorganized, self-alienated, morally and ideologically disarmed. They lack leadership; the Hindu elites have become illiterate about their spiritual heritage and history and indifferent and even hostile towards their religion.... India's higher education, its academia and media are in the hands of a Hindu-hating elite.

Note what Ram Swarup has to say of the caste system: 'Once when Hinduism was strong, castes represented a *natural* and healthy diversity, but now in its present state of weakness these are used for its dismemberment. Old vested interests joined by new ones have come together to make use of the caste factor in a big way in order to keep Hindus down.'

Sikhs are not spared. Ram Swarup adopts a dual approach in *Hindu-Sikh Relationship* (1985). He woos them as 'the members of Hindu society' and denounces them for thinking that 'they were different.' Base motives are freely attributed: 'Thanks to the Green Revolution and various other factors, the Sikhs have become relatively more rich and prosperous. No wonder, they have begun to find that the Hindu bond is not good enough for them and they seek a new identity readily available to them in their names and outer symbols. This is an understandable human frailty.'

He defends the storming of the Golden Temple. It 'became an arsenal, a fort, a sanctuary for criminals. This grave situation called for necessary action which caused some *unavoidable* damage to the building.' There followed 'protest meetings, resolutions', which he deprecates. 'The whole thing created widespread resentment all over India which burst into a most unwholesome violence when Mrs. Indira Gandhi was assassinated. A growing resentment at the arrogant

Akali politics is the main cause of this fearful happening.'

This is of a piece with the *Organiser's* defence of Gandhi's assassination in its editorial (January 11, 1970) – 'turned the people's wrath on himself.'

Sita Ram Goel's ardour is reflected in his three books *Catholic Ashrams, Papacy* and *History of Hindu-Christian Encounters.* His preface to the second edition (1996) of the book on Hindu–Christian encounters explains a lot:

> The Sangh *parivar*, which had turned cold towards Hindu causes over the years, *was startled by the rout of the Bharatiya Janata Party in the 1984 elections, and decided to renew its Hindu character. The Ramajanmabhoomi Movement was the result.* The Movement was aimed at arresting Islamic aggression. Christianity or its missions were hardly mentioned. Nevertheless, it was Christianity which showed the greatest concern at this new Hindu stir, and started crying 'wolf'. Its media power in the West raised a storm, saying that Hindus were out to destroy the minorities in India and impose a Nazi regime. The storm is still raging and no one knows when it will subside, if at all.

Thus 'the storm' was unleashed for reasons of power through election victories.

Goel's writings alone prove that the *parivar's* ire against Christians is decades old. In an article published in March 1983 he had asserted that the ancient Hindu precept *sarva dharma samabhava* (all religions are equal) should not be applied to Christians or Muslims.

It is with some hesitation that one turns to Goel's book *Jesus Christ An Artifice for Aggression* (1994); so wantonly offensive is it. The focus now is not on the missionaries, or politics, or history. The target is the faith itself; Christianity as a religion. Why? Because hitherto

> we Hindus have remained occupied with the behaviour patterns of Muslims and Christians and not with the belief systems which create those behaviour patterns. We object to Christian missions, but refuse to discuss Christianity and its God, Jesus. We object to Islamic terrorisms, but refuse to have a look at Islam and its prophet, Muhammad. I see no sense or logic in this Hindu habit.

Is there any other country in the world where such theses are written for such a purpose? One wonders. 'Now, I could see why the history of Christianity had been what it had been. The source of the poison was in the Jesus of the gospels.'

The Immaculate Conception of Virgin Mary is attacked wantonly. There are chapters on Jesus of history, of fiction and of faith. The thesis? He did not exist in history.

> The quantum of crimes committed by Muhammad's Islam was only slightly smaller than that of the crimes committed by the Christianity of the Jesus Christ. . . . The parallel between Jesus and Hitler was seen as still more striking. The Nazi creed, as laid down by Hitler, did not sound much different from the Christian creed as preached by Jesus in the gospels.

Goel is dismayed to find that Jesus Christ 'should continue to retain his hallow' (*sic*) in India. 'Christianity is accepted as a religion not only by the westernized Hindu elite but also by Hindu saints, scholars, and political platforms.'

Jesus Christ has been 'praised to the skies, particularly by Mahatma Gandhi.' But,

> it is high time for Hindus to learn that Jesus Christ symbolizes no spiritual power, or moral uprightness. He is no more than an artifice for legitimizing wanton imperialist aggression. The aggressors have found him to be highly profitable so far. By the same token, Hindus should know that Jesus means nothing but mischief for their country and culture. The West where he flourished for long has discarded him as junk. There is no reason why Hindus should buy him. He is the type of junk that cannot be re-cycled. He can only poison the environment.

The virulence of the language reveals the depths of the hatred. This is what Indians are up against – a powerful hate group, enjoying the patronage of many politicians in power and in the administration, which is out to wipe out all traces not only of secularism and democracy but of religious tolerance, religious and cultural diversity and, indeed, of decency itself from India.

It shall not come to pass.

THE RSS AND CONSTITUTION OF INDIA

The Sangh *parivar* published its 'White Paper' denouncing the Constitution as 'anti-Hindu' and outlining the kind of polity it wishes to establish in the country on January 1, 1993. Its front cover posed two questions: 'Who is the destroyer of India's integrity, brotherhood and communal amity?' and 'Who has spread starvation, unemployment, corruption and irreligion?' The answer is provided in the title of the White Paper – '*Vartaman* Indian *Samvidhan*'.[2]

The word 'Indian' has been used in the Hindi title with a purpose. The implication is that it is an *Indian* rather than *Hindu* Constitution. That is its central theme. In the foreword, Swami Hiranand writes: 'The present Constitution is contrary to the country's culture, character, circumstances, situation, etc. It is foreign-oriented.' Commending the document to the reader, he concludes: 'We will have to think afresh about our economic policy, judicial and administrative structure and other national institutions *only* after nullifying the present Constitutions.' It has to be discarded completely as a matter of high priority: 'The damage done by two hundred years long rule of the British is negligible as compared to the harm done by our Constitution. The conspiracy to convert Bharat into India continues.' He laments that 'we are known as Indians the world over' and reminds the reader that 'the freedom struggle was fought in the name of Hindustan. Vande Mataram was our national song . . . in post-Independence India, Hindustan and Vande Mataram have been exterminated. Jana Gana Mana, a song to welcome George V, has become our national anthem.'

The pamphlet was not a sudden outburst. It was a calculated move, made after full deliberation. On December 25, 1992, soon after the demolition of the Babri Masjid, its author Swami Muktanand held a press conference in New Delhi, *at the residence of a BJP Member of Parliament*, jointly with Swami Vamdeo Maharaj. They gave a call to the nation to reject the 'anti-Hindu Constitution': 'We have no faith in the country's laws' and 'the sadhus are above the law of the land.' India's citizenship law which considers all born in the country as its natural citizens is 'humbug'. A week later, Muktanand's pamphlet was published.

Fittingly enough, the mother of the *parivar*, the RSS, was the first to express its views on the White Paper. In January 1993 the then *de facto* RSS supremo, Rajendra Singh wrote:

> The present conflict can be partially attributed to the inadequacies of
> our system in responding to the needs of the essential India, its tradition,
> values and ethos. . . . Certain specialties of this country should be reflected

in the Constitution. In place of 'India that is Bharat,' we should have said 'Bharat that is Hindustan.' Official documents refer to the 'composite culture,' but ours is certainly not a composite culture. Culture is not wearing of clothes or speaking languages. In a very fundamental sense, this country has a unique cultural oneness. No country, if it has to survive, can have compartments. All this shows that changes are needed in the Constitution. *A Constitution more suited to the ethos and genius of this country should be adopted in the future.* (*IE* January 14, 1993)

On January 24 at Anantapur, Andhra Pradesh, M.M. Joshi, then BJP President, 'reiterated the demand for a fresh look at the Constitution.' Thus, far from being disowned, Muktanand's pamphlet has been confirmed in the *parivar*'s distinctive style – creep stealthily, make ambiguous formulations which are followed by explicit assertions.

The entire *parivar* is fundamentally illiberal, anti-intellectual and rejects the Western intellectual tradition. The pamphlet complains: 'Westernized people unfamiliar with the culture and history of India are the creators of our Constitution.' The pamphlet condemns reservations for the Scheduled Castes, Scheduled Tribes and Backward Classes. The minorities fare worse. The Constitution is denounced in intemperate language. 'This Constitution can be called a pile of garbage . . . the Constitution of India is an enemy of the nation's unity and integrity.'

THE RSS AND THE SERVICES

On November 4, 1948, while introducing the draft Constitution in the Constituent Assembly, Ambedkar expounded the fundamentals underlying it: 'The form of the administration must be appropriate and in the same sense as the form of the Constitution.' An RSS-ridden civil service cannot work a secular Constitution. For, 'it is perfectly possible to pervert the Constitution without changing its form, by merely changing the form of the administration and to [*sic*] make it inconsistent and opposed to the spirit of the Constitution.' On October 10, 1949, Home Minister Patel had echoed these views: 'If you do not adopt this course, then do not follow the present Constitution. Put in a Congress Constitution or some other Constitution or put in the RSS Constitution – whatever you like – but not this Constitution. This Constitution is meant to be worked by a ring of service which will keep the country intact.' Earlier, on April 27, 1948, he had written to Nehru:

I need hardly emphasize that an efficient, disciplined and contented service, assured of its prospect as a result of diligent and honest work, is a sine qua non of sound administration under a democratic regime even more than under an authoritarian rule. The service must be above party and we should ensure that political considerations, either in its recruitment or in its discipline and control, are reduced to the minimum, if not eliminated altogether.

The exact opposite of this was done by the Gujarat government with the full backing of current union Home Minister Advani. Ever since Independence, governments at the Centre and in the states banned members of certain organizations from recruitment to their respective services. Additionally, they forbade personnel of the services from membership of those bodies. The list was prepared by the Centre and revised periodically; the last time, in 1986. Accordingly, the Gujarat Civil Servants Conduct Rules, 1971, forbade them from having any connection with the RSS. Among the other 16 organizations on that list were the VHP, Hindu Mahasabha, Anand Marg, All-India Muslim Majlis-e-Mushawarat, Sati Pati Creed and Mass Movement (Madhok faction).

The change was brought about with a deviousness and disingenuity that reveals the Advani approach in its true colours. The Gujarat government sent a 'query' to the union Home Ministry, quite out of the blue, and the latter sent the desired reply. What was the inspiration behind this move in respect of just one blacklisted body? There was not even the pretence of a comprehensive review of the list by the Centre. The state RSS had organized a mammoth camp of 30,000 near Ahmedabad from January 7. Gujarat's Home Minister Haren Pandya disclosed the contents of the Centre's letter of July 13, 1999. It cited the report of the Unlawful Activities Tribunal in 1993 which had not found anything 'unlawful' in RSS activities.

This was a reference to the report of the tribunal, headed by Justice P.K. Bahri of the Delhi High Court, on June 4, 1993, under the Unlawful Activities (Prevention) Act, 1967, striking down the Government of India's order of December 10, 1992 banning the RSS along with the VHP and the Bajrang Dal. The bans, imposed after the demolition of the Babri Masjid on December 6, cited two grounds, namely, complicity in the demolition and imputation of disloyalty against members of certain communities. This ban, surely, had nothing to do with the blacklist of old which was based on wider considerations which are still valid. If the letter of July 13 had passed muster, there was nothing to prevent Advani from amending the Central Civil Services (Conduct) Rules, 1994 on the lines of the Gujarat amendment.

For the first time ever members of the Armed forces were dragged into the RSS's politics, as Praveen Swami has recorded:

> The rise of the Hindu right to power was anticipated by the systematic infiltration of the highest levels of the Army apparatus. While the bulk of the Army leadership remains avowedly apolitical, the BJP has made methodical efforts to subvert this tradition, dragging a section of senior officers on to expressly partisan terrain. The decision of Director-General of Military Operations M.C. Vij and Air Vice Marshall S.K. Malik to brief the BJP National Executive on the Kargil war on May 6 is just one example of this process. 3 Infantry Division commander Major-General Budhwar helped provide logistical support for the RSS-organized Sindhu Darshan festival at Leh in 1998. Advani and ideologue Tarun Vijay were among those who attended. In 1999, he again attended the Sindhu Darshan, organized with official aid, and graced by Vajpayee, Fernandes and Advani. Asked by a journalist whether it was appropriate for him to associate with political organizations, Budhwar claimed not to understand the question.[3]

Murli Manohar Joshi, Union Minister for Human Resources Development, has been as assiduous as Advani in pursuing the *Parivar*'s agenda. An unprecedented uproar at the Education Minsters' Conference, on October 22, 1998, over the attempt to saffronise the syllabus did not deter him. In 1999 he appointed M.L. Sondhi, an academic who was a former Jan Sangh M.P., as Chairperson of the Indian Council of Social Science Research and B.R. Grover, who had helped in 'discovery' of a temple at Ayodhya in ancient times, as Chairperson of the Indian Council of Historical Research. Under Grover the ICHR lost little time in trying to saffronise the writing of history as well. As member of the ICHR he had written to the HRD ministry asking it to stop funds to the ICHR because it had been criticizing 'their policies on one count or another.' Grover had the manuscripts of Professors K.N. Panikkar and Sumit Sarkar in the *Towards Freedom* Project recalled for vetting.

8

EPILOGUE:
RETROSPECT AND PROSPECT

At the end of his visit to Kathmandu, External Affairs minister Jaswant Singh was asked at a press conference, on September 12, 1999, whether his trip in the midst of a general election reflected a 'Hindu' BJP's special gesture towards a 'Hindu' country. Incensed, Jaswant Singh replied: 'The label of a "Hindu" party only indicates the mind of a person who uses such a label.'

The remark was far truer than he realized. The *Organiser* of August 5, 1989 quoted the then BJP President Advani proudly saying to the BBC: 'It would not be wrong to call [the] BJP a Hindu party' Advani has consistently espoused the Savarkar–Golwalkar thesis on 'cultural nationalism.' The BJP's Manifesto for the 1996 election to the Lok Sabha said: 'The BJP is committed to the concept of one nation, one people, one culture. . . . From this belief flows our faith in "Cultural Nationalism" which is the core of Hindutva. . . . Hindutva is a unifying principle which alone can preserve the unity and integrity of our nation.' Its Manifesto for the 1998 elections reiterated the credo: 'The cultural nationalism of India . . . is the core of Hindutva.' Only a couple of months later, the BJP omitted this and two other controversial issues in the National Agenda for Governance which it adopted with its allies, on March 18, 1998, in order to acquire a majority in the Lok Sabha and form a government; namely, abnegation of Article 370 of the constitution conferring a special status on the state of Jammu and Kashmir and enactment of a uniform civil code. The BJP did not issue a Manifesto for the 1999 elections; only subscribed to one by the National Democratic Alliance it had concluded with the allies.

This has led to a debate on whether it has 'a hidden agenda.' Public memory is proverbially short. On May 28, 1996 Atal Behari Vajpayee had in desperation offered to 'freeze' the three issues in order to avert certain defeat in the Lok Sabha on the vote of confidence in his short-lived government. If the offer of a 'freeze' in 1996 did not deter the BJP from issuing its 1998 Manifesto, there is no reason to believe that its silence on them now is anything but a tactical and temporary concession dictated by the compulsions of power.

Three factors reinforce this view. Men who expounded an outlook so unequivocally and for so long over the last fifty years are unlikely to change their views, even if expediency dictates silence. Secondly, the BJP is haplessly dependent on the RSS. The parent is realistic to recognize that it, too, stands to gain if its offspring remains in power. But there is a point beyond which the RSS will not permit the BJP to compromise its ideology. It will deploy others in the family – the VHP and the Bajrang Dal – to bring the BJP to heel. Lastly, even during these trying moments since 1998 the BJP has been so evasive as to suggest calculated deceit.

Consider, for instance, the statement made by K.S. Sudarshan soon after being appointed the RSS supremo in March 2000: 'We are creating an atmosphere, through public awakening in which not only the Vajpayee Government but any government that comes to power will have to accept our thinking' (*Outlook*, March 27, 2000). Earlier, in 1999, when many BJP activists resented the omission to publish a separate election manifesto, RSS sources said: 'Our priority is to install a BJP-led government at the Centre. But that does not mean that it will be done at the cost of our agenda. It is very much there without any dilution . . . it will be the BJP alone which is going to implement our agenda' (*AA* August 18, 1999).

The BJP's General Secretary, K.N. Govindacharya, said on August 22, 1999: 'We work with a bifocal vision. We are neither breaking out of our commitment to those [three] issues nor are we apologetic about our stand. *With the BJP yet to traverse some more distance to attain the steering position in Indian politics we decided*

*that in this interregnum of transition we should commit ourselves to
the document of the national agenda for governance formulated on
the basis of consensus* among all partners of NDA'. He said explicitly
that the BJP 'is committed to the three contentious issues.' Kalraj
Mishra, then a senior minister in the Uttar Pradesh government,
echoed this line. 'Elections or no election, the party was committed
to the construction of Ram Temple'. Vajpayee tried damage control:
'We are fighting on the NDA manifesto and all contentious issues
should not be brought into the political arena.' Advani, however,
asserted that they *remained* on the BJP's agenda though 'for a coalition
government idealism is more important than ideology.'

Neena Vyas of *The Hindu* noted how in one day alone (August
25) the BJP 'continued to talk in different voices on the Ram temple
issue' with M. Venkaiah Naidu contradicting Kalraj Mishra. Two days
later, Ramu Bhagwat reported from Nagpur: 'the RSS realizes that
getting Mr Vajpayee back into power is much more important.'
Mamasaheb Ghumre, former Vice-President of the VHP told him
that 'the temple issue has a better chance of getting built with him in
the saddle for five years.' Govindacharya stuck to his line on September
4: 'Our moratorium is *for five years* which is the term of the
forthcoming Lok Sabha.'

At the BJP's National Council at Chennai, Advani assured
members on December 29: '*There is no question of our party discard-
ing its ideology.* Don't be apologetic about it.' BJP Vice-President Jana
Krishnamurthy reiterated this on January 13, 2000 while releasing
the 20-page Chennai Declaration: 'The BJP has not in any manner
compromised on its basic identity.' A sentence in the first draft – 'the
BJP has no agenda other than the common agenda of the NDA' –
had caused a revolt and was deleted. It reappeared in the six-page
'highlights' of the Declaration also released that day, 'by mistake'!

THE NEW FUHRER

On March 10, 2000, the RSS recast its National Executive. Kuppahali
Seetaramaiyah Sudarshan was appointed its supremo, Sarsanghchalak, in succession to Rajendra Singh who stepped down but vowed
to continue to 'guide' the Sangh. He had served in the post for six
years. Mohan Madhukarrao Bhagwat replaced H.V. Seshadri as
Sarkaryavah, General Secretary. Seshadri became Joint General

Secretary, Sahsarkaryavah. Rajendra Singh was not, however, made a member of the Executive but ranked among five invitees to its meetings.

The very day after his appointment, Sudarshan said that despite pressure from the allies, the Vajpayee Government was in favour of constructing the Ram temple at Ayodhya. On economic matters, he advised, 'The Prime Minister should bring in economic advisers who believe in the swadeshi concept.' He also demanded that the Constitution of India be scrapped. This 'remake of the British model in [sic] 1935' should be replaced with one based on the 'aspirations of the people.' In drafting the present Constitution 'Indian ethos and aspirations were not taken into account.' He added that 'the RSS did not expect the Review Committee to do this [take a fresh look] as it has been asked not to alter the basic structure of the Constitution'.

On the same day, March 11, in his first address to RSS activists in Nagpur, Sudarshan said: 'These non-Hindus are not foreigners but ex-Hindus; they are·Indians but their faiths will have to be Indianized.' He repeated this admonition in New Delhi on March 23: 'This is yet another epic war – between Hindus and anti-Hindus, a veritable Mahabharat in which sometime Abhimanyu will fall, sometime Ghatotkacha or it may be Jayadratha's turn yet another day. . . . This is Hindu Rashtra. It is based on dharma. Its identity lies in one Motherland, one sanskriti, common ancestry and heritage and the unity in diversity. It is these three that constitute the national culture. The mode of worship can differ from person to person' (*Organiser* March 19, 2000).

He attacked Gandhi as well as Nehru. 'Even Gandhi blamed the Hindu community for creating an environment congenial to communal conflicts.' He asserted that 'third phase in RSS history was marked by Jawaharlal Nehru's efforts to curb the organization' (*Organiser* March 19). The demolition of the Babri Masjid, he claimed on March 19, 'has made Hindus all over the world proud.' For a man who extols the use of violence, his language is befittingly coarse and vulgar. 'Intellectual is that class of bastards, which tries to implant an alien culture in their land', he said on March 17.

Sudarshan is a man on the move. Sanjay Basak's report of March 17 says: 'With a friendly government at the Centre, the RSS intends to step up its activities for the "creation for a Hindu rashtra." The RSS is likely to start the process of finalizing its "blue-print" on the

Hindu philosophy in June and will submit it to the government for consideration.' Sudarshan has promised an 'explosion of Hindutva.'

Elated at his elevation, Sudarshan launched on a lecture tour with great enthusiasm, to the embarrassment of the BJP Government. His references to 'Sindhu' must have endeared him to Advani after his excursions to Leh. On April 29 at Chandigarh, Sudarshan advocated the undoing of the partition by annexing Pakistan:

> At the appropriate time, we will form Akhand Bharat [United India]. *We have to regain the areas which we lost in 1947.* We have to regain Lahore – the Capital of Maharaja Ranjit Singh's Khalsa Raj. We have to reclaim Nankana Sahib and several other religious places, as also Sindhu [Indus] and Kasoor. The feeling for 'Akhand Bharat' has to survive because it is akin to the feeling that led to the unification of Germany, Vietnam and Poland [*sic*]. Partition of India was wrong. (*TS* April 30, 2000)

The paper's report continued: 'Asserting that India was a Hindu "Rashtra", Mr Sudarshan said Hindu in this context referred to the nationality and added that there were many religions in India and the correct translation for this term in Hindi was not "dharma" but "panth" or "sampradaya."' This was the classic RSS double talk of old practised by Deoras and Golwalkar. All who live in India are 'Hindus' it claims at times; yet refuses to enroll non-Hindus as members and constantly speaks of the Hindus as India's 'majority community' which has been wronged by its minorities.

Sudarshan was addressing the Rashtriya Sikh Sangat. Over a dozen Sikh organizations held a protest demonstration alleging an 'RSS agenda of assimilation of Sikhs into Hinduism and demanding a ban on the RSS,' *The Statesman* reported. The controversy had lain dormant. Sudarshan revived it. Even the Shiromani Akali Dal attacked the RSS for trying 'to infiltrate into Sikh religion.' Kanwarpal Singh of Dal Khalsa was less polite. He called the Rashtriya Sikh Sangat 'a bastard child of the RSS' (*AA* April 30).

Meanwhile, attacks on the Christians continued unabated. The late Archbishop of Delhi Alan de Lastic, wrote to Prime Minister Vajpayee once again in May 2000 drawing his attention to it: 'But there has been no response to the appeal from the Prime Minister's Office,' Seema Mustafa reported (*AA* May 14). The All-India Christian Council laid the blame for the spurt in the attacks squarely

where it belonged – the Government of India. 'We are intrigued by
the response of the Central and State governments who refuse to see
the pattern of the violence,' its President Dr Joseph D'Souza said on
June 16 at Chennai. The Bajrang Dal's Gauleiter (Sah-Sahayojak)
for the Braj region, Dharmendra Sharma, declared that the Christians
are now 'bigger enemies' than Muslims. 'We are prepared to use
violence [against church bodies]. There is no limit', Siddharth
Varadarajan reported from Mathura, shortly after the murder of
Brother George there and the attack at Kosikalan on Father Thomas.
'Local Bajrang Dal leaders make no bones about their intention to
drive "Christians away from the State."' (*TOI* June 3, 2000).

The Chairman of the National Human Rights Commission,
Justice J.S. Verma, former Chief Justice of India, hit upon a simple
test which showed up the Sangh *parivar*. On June 30, he asked the
VHP and the Bajrang Dal leaders 'to tell their activists, whose names
have appeared as having made inciting statements, to deny the charges
publicly. And, if they refuse to do so, then the organizations should
denounce them.' (*HT* July 1). The VHP's Vice-President Giriraj
Kishore reacted at once, by warmly praising the Bajrang Dal the very
next day. The BJP's General Secretary K.N. Govindacharya said on
July 9: 'The Church is in collusion with militants and is supporting
ethnic cleansing of Hindus in the north-eastern States' (*TT* July 10).
This allegation, so patently false, was made at Lucknow just when
the atmosphere in the entire State (Uttar Pradesh) was being poisoned
against the Christians. It was of a piece with the VHP's General
Secretary Pravin Togadia's threat in Mumbai on August 4 that it
would retaliate if the Hindus in Kashmir were killed by 'Islamic
fundamentalist group'.

It does suit the RSS to have a BJP Government in power at the
Centre. But the clock is ticking away against both. Of what use a BJP
regime to the RSS if it does not implement the RSS agenda? If the
BJP continues as it is, domesticated and rendered 'respectable', the
political arm of the RSS will be atrophied and its agenda forgotten, if
not discredited. That leaves infiltration in the administration,
saffronization of education and imposition of cultural hegemony as
possible fields of endeavour.

But if the BJP listens to the RSS on these matters, it loses allies
and alienates public opinion. If it does not, it loses the RSS's support.
Whom is it prepared now to deceive and ditch, the RSS or the nation

whom it keeps assuring that it has no 'hidden agenda' apart from that of the NDA? The BJP is confronted with a dilemma of its own creation.

Which is why, on April 19, 2000, the VHP leader Acharya Dharmendra Maharaj charged Vajpayee with showing 'undue haste' to become Prime Minister, 'damaging' the cause of Hindutva in the process. The BJP should have waited for a couple of years 'after which it would have won a clear majority on its own. *Lekin Atalji ko jaldi thee* [But Atalji was in a hurry to become Prime Minster].' The BJP, he added, was a 'political company' floated by the Sangh *parivar* and it had now gone bankrupt.

The parent company is itself not very much in good fortune, either. The demolition of the Babri Masjid in 1992 has cost the RSS dearly. Electoral successes on the strength of the Hindutva slogan have only brought the Sangh *parivar* face to face with the old dilemma – shed the ideology or shed power. With the RSS's momentary tolerance, the BJP has been trying to retain power while speaking with a forked tongue on its ideology. No one is amused by the act. For, this is not a tight-rope walk, accepted in the robust Indian performance tradition. It is a strip-tease which reflects 'the decadent culture of the West', abhorrent to the RSS.

REVIVING THE TEMPLE ISSUE

Out of the blue came Vajpayee's revival of the temple issue; first in New York on September 9, 2000, and then in Delhi, three months later. On the former occasion, Vajpayee tore apart more then one *mukhota* (mask). The RSS chief K.S. Sudarshan, VHP leaders Ashok Singhal, Acharya Giriraj Kishore and B.K. Modi 'had taken personal interest in organizing this function where the Prime Minister of India was to be brought into contact with the saints, swamis and VHP cadres' (*AA* September 12).

Vajpayee was fully conscious of the political complexion of the audience and organizers. He said: 'I will not always remain Prime Minister; there are plenty of people for the job in Delhi. But my right to remain a Swayamsevak can not be taken away.'

In reply to a pointed question by Swamy Satyanand, 'when a Ram temple would be built in Ayodhya,' Vajpayee said 'if the electorate gives us a clear two-thirds majority, we will build the India of our dreams. There is not doubt about that' (*TS* September 11). It was an explicit pledge in response to an explicit question. Vajpayee indicated to his audience, and indeed to the nation as well, all too clearly that he shares the Sangh *parivar*'s dream. The masks are off – from his face and that of the BJP as well.

It took Vajpayee over 48 hours to deny what all the correspondents had reported in identical terms. His explanation was facile. He claimed that he meant only volunteer (swayamsevak) of the country. The expression swayamsevak of the country, however, simply does not belong to India's political language. As the French say, nothing is convincing that requires elaborately to be explained.

The RSS chief, on his part, sounded a stern warning on his annual Vijayadashmi speech soon after (October 7, 2000). He made two points, only one of which was reported: 'We need to have an Indian national church for the Indian Christians.' Only a few months before, Vajpayee had met the Pope in Rome. It is only a matter of time before Indian Muslims are instructed not to go on the Haj pilgrimage.

What went unreported was the following cameo. Sudarshan said that

> the condition of Hindus in different parts of the world depends upon the condition of Hindus in India. The stronger the Hindus are in India the more secure the Hindus in other parts of the world feel themselves. Calling upon Hindus to *be armed for their self-defence*, [Sudarshan] pointed out that the Sangh work, started by Dr Hedgewar in 1925 has now *attained global presence*. Besides India, there are more than 35 countries of the world that have Sangh shakhas [branches]. It includes 60 shakhas in the US, 70 in England, 11 in Holland, 18 in Trinidad, 11 in Surinam, and 4 in Guyana.

RSS renewed its hard line at a mammoth conclave on 'national security' at Agra (October 13–15, 2000). It threatened the NDA government with 'consequences' if it obstructed construction of a temple at Ayodhya. On October 15, Sudarshan asked Muslims and Christians, in Advani's presence, to return to 'Hindu roots.'

In New Delhi, on October 17, Advani admitted that 'the RSS exercises a moral influence on the government.' The RSS General Secretary Mohan Bhagwat told *Organiser* (October 22, 2000): 'Politics has never been considered an untouchable area by the swayamsevaks.'

It became clear that Vajpayee's remarks in New York were not made off-the-cuff, after all. The RSS and the VHP brought the Ram temple issue to the fore calculatedly, provocatively. The BJP encouraged them while making, at the same time, reassuring gestures to its allies in the NDA who needed just about enough to save face in order to stay in power.

The three arms of the Sangh parivar acted in impressive concert. Bangaru Laxman, while claiming that the BJP was not following the RSS's ideology, still acknowledged that 'the RSS is a moral force for the BJP.' He added: 'but it is not necessary that it [the BJP] should accept each and everything said by the RSS' (*TOI* October 24, 2000).

The degree of RSS influence over the BJP and the government it led soon became evident. It was bared to all by none other than Vajpayee on the eighth anniversary of the demolition of the Babri Masjid, in successive statements on December 6, 7 and 13. As he later acknowledged on January 5, 2001, at the BJP's National Executive meeting, those remarks were 'well thought-out' ('*Sab soch samajh ke kaha*') (*TH* January 6, 2001).

Vajpayee has always been ambiguous on the temple issue. In 1991, he claimed that the construction of a Ram temple at Ayodhya was necessary 'to save the honour of the Hindu community' (May 12). However, he offered to 'freeze' the issue, along with two others (May 28), to save his short-lived government in 1996; and did so, again, in 1998 and 1999 to form one. Sushma Swaraj was right when she said in Bhopal, on April 14, 2000, that the temple movement was 'purely political in nature and had nothing to do with religion.'

On December 1, 2000, Vajpayee hosted a dinner for the top brass of the RSS, including K. Sudarshan, general secretary Mohan Bhagwat, former and present BJP presidents, Kushabhau Thakre and Bangaru Laxman respectively, and L.K. Advani. Vajpayee's statement on 6 December was made against this background quite calculatedly. 'The project for constructing a Ram temple in Ayodhya was the expression of *nationalist* feelings. The work has not yet been completed.' This was said after the Lok Sabha had been adjourned for the third consecutive day on the issue. Kushabhau Thakre confirmed that Vajpayee spoke 'in a planned way' (*TH* December 14, 2000). Evidently the line had been laid down at the strategy session over dinner and Vajpayee was carrying it out faithfully.

The Supreme Court has unanimously rejected the view that it was a 'nationalist' project. Two judges (A.M. Ahmadi and S.P. Bharuchi J.J.) did so, explicitly citing the prior existence of the demolished Babri Masjid. The others (M.N. Venkatachaliah C.J., and J.S. Verma and G.N. Ray J.J.) did so implicitly. (*Ismail Faruqui and Ors. vs. Union of India and Ors.* (1994) 6 Supreme Court Cases 360.) Section 4 (3) of the Ayodhya Acquisition Act, 1993 was struck down precisely because it aborted a litigation between two sides comprising different communities. A Prime Minister who characterizes the demand of the one, the majority, as 'nationalist', violates his oath of office, which binds him to hold the scales evenly, the factual falsehood apart. *A fortiori* when he commits himself to completion of that communal project. His second assertion that the three ministers (Advani, Joshi, and Uma Bharti) were there 'to protect it and not to demolish it' is manifestly untrue. It is, in any case, a matter for the sessions court to decide, not him. What he is bound to, in all propriety, is to remove them till the court, which has framed the charges, delivers its verdict. Evidently, Vajpayee shares their apprehensions of its verdict.

The following day (December 7), Vajpayee again approximated a communal demand as a national one, with equal deliberation and disregard for the truth. He said: 'The entire country wants the temple. The Muslims do not oppose it. The issue is how to make it and where' (*TS* December 8). Vajpayee was quite clear in his mind that the mosque 'can be built *elsewhere*.' This was his basis for 'a negotiated settlement' (*TT* December 8). The VHP instantly welcomed his remarks and revealed that 5,000 cubic feet of completed stonework had been dispatched to Ayodhya on lorries the day before. It is unlikely that Vajpayee was unaware of this.

In parliament, on December 14, Vajpayee reiterated, for the third time, deliberately, his formulation of December 6 and 7 – construction of a Ram temple at Ayodhya was 'connected with national sentiment. How can you take exception to it? Can't a temple be built on the basis of national sentiment?' (*IE* December 15, 2000).

It is unnecessary to discuss the pathetically disingenuous parallels he drew with the Dargah at Ajmer and the Golden Temple at Amritsar, since Vajpayee himself claimed on April 6, 1989: '*Hindus* were the rightful claimants of the site.' He added that he spoke not as a BJP leader, but as an RSS swayamsevak and a Hindu. Vajpayee's denial in the Rajya Sabha on December 19 that he asked for the rebuilding of a temple at the site of the demolished mosque is belied by his statement on December 7 quoted above. It is insulting to say that Muslims are prepared to accept such a humiliating proposal. Nor is it a concession that he now agrees to abide by a court order; for, the Supreme Court ruling completely bars a legislative fiat which the BJP had demanded hitherto.

On December 14, the Lok Sabha defeated an opposition motion on the subject by 291 votes to 179. Vajpayee not only rejected the demand for the resignation of Advani, Joshi, and Uma Bharati, but asked rhetorically: 'Can't a temple be built on the basis of *national sentiment?*'

To Bangaru Laxman this meant endorsement of the *parivar's* stand on the temple. 'Parliament has endorsed the view that the temple cannot be moved.' He was referring to the fact that the Rao government had deliberately refrained from removing from the site of the demolished mosque the idols planted there in a ramshackle temple, as Jyoti Basu had demanded. Laxman asserted: 'it would be difficult to remove the Ram temple from there *despite an adverse court verdict'* (*IE* December 16, 2000)

The Rajya Sabha adopted a censure motion on December 19 by 121 votes to 86, the first in two decades. On the same day, the VHP chief Ashok Singhal made bold to own up that at Ayodhya on December 6, 1992, 'thousands of kar sevaks were present there *with the clear intention of demolishing the mosque'* (*HT* December 20, 2000). Five days later, he declared: 'We have decided to build temples to Bharat, Laxman and Hanuman because we do not want any masjid to come up close to the Ram temple' (*TT* December 25, 2000).

Thus, Vajpayee's remarks had served only to stoke the fires of Hindutva. The BJP's Vice President, Pyarelal Khandelwal, affirmed on December 28 that the temple issue remained on the BJP's agenda (*TH* December 29, 2000). Bangaru Laxman confirmed this, and more, with crystal clarity. The BJP had not at all given up the triple contentious issues of a Ram temple, Uniform Civil Code and abrogation of Article 370. 'We have not given them up. They are still in our policy documents although we have not kept them in our common agenda [of the NDA]. We have never said that we will throw these policy documents in the dustbin' (*TH* February 25, 2001).

In his famous Kumarkom Musings, Vajpayee did nothing to improve the situation. Indeed, he could not. It was a calculated strategy that he had adopted, in concert with the RSS, with an eye to the elections to the Uttar Pradesh assembly due before long, not to forget possible mid-term poll to the Lok Sabha.

On the other hand, he had to also reckon with the criticism his
remarks had aroused universally outside the ranks of the Sangh
parivar. He said that there were 'only two ways to resolve this
contentious issue: the judicial route or the route of negotiations leading
to a mutually acceptable solution.' He explained:

> In my reply to the debate in the Rajya Sabha, I had clearly stated that
> although the movement for the construction of a Ram Temple at Ayodhya
> was an expression of our national sentiment, this sentiment became
> narrow, and its inclusive character became restrictive, because of the
> unfortunate demolition of the disputed mosque structure on December
> 6, 1992. A flagrant violation of the law, it certainly was. But it was also
> totally at variance with the Hindu ethos. The wrongs of a medieval past
> cannot be righted by a similar wrong in modern times. The status quo
> at Kashi, Mathura and other disputed places of worship must remain
> undisturbed. [*HT* January 3, 2001]

On January 10, 2001, the VHP magnanimously granted the
government a year's reprieve. The decision was taken at 'a top-level
meeting at the RSS headquarters' which was attended by Sudarshan
and VHP Vice-President Giriraj Kishore (*TOI* January 11, 2001).
The RSS spokesman, M.G. Vaidya, was precise: 'Construction of the
Ram temple can be started either on Ram's birthday [Ram Navmi in
April], before the gods go to sleep during Christmas, or on Devothan
Ekadashi [in November], when they wake up' (*IE* January 12, 2001).
That meant either November 26, 2001 or April 2002.

It is a most disturbing situation. For, the VHP has resolved 'to
create a band of about 1 million militant cadres with the *trishul*
[trident] committed to build the Ram temple in Ayodhya in 2002.
This will be in addition to the 2 million people the VHP will recruit
through the Bajrang Dal. About 3,00,000 will get special training',
The Statesman reported on January 26 in a detailed exposé of fund-
raising and muscle-building. (Vide also *The Hindu*, January 26,
2001.) Meanwhile, on January 25, 2001, the VHP Dharam Sansad
put the imprimatur of its approval on the January 10 decision and
declared March 12, 2002 as the deadline (*TOI* January 25, 2001).

But there was also another clock that was ticking away and its
chimes on February 12, 2001 took every one by surprise. Justice Jagdish
Bhalla of the Lucknow Bench of the Allahabad High Court upheld

the validity of the CBI's charge-sheet and the magistrate's committal order in the demolition case on the main charges of conspiracy for and actual demolition (Case No. 197). He struck down, both, in respect of a charge against Advani, Joshi, Bharati and five other politicians (Case No. 198) concerning the speeches delivered on December 6, 1992, just prior to the demolition. This was because of a procedural flaw which he stressed was 'curable'. He censured the delays and urged the need for despatch.[1]

It is an arrogant and ambitiously evangelical mindset, which prompts the RSS to speak and act in a manner that arouses dread in its victims, ridicule in the observers, and contempt in everyone. The RSS General Secretary Mohan Bhagwat proclaimed at Nagpur on January 2, 2001, to Hindu Swayamsevaks who had collected at Nagpur from 38 countries from all over the world, that 'god has given the Hindus the responsibility to take the peoples of the world to the pinnacle of human glory. . . . The whole world [is] looking at India with hope' (*IE* January 3, 2001)

According to the RSS, Homer adapted Valmiki's *Ramayana* into his *Iliad*, while Jesus Christ roamed across the Himalayas and drew his ideas from Hinduism. These historical discoveries and many more figure in text books taught in RSS-run schools (*TT* November 18, 2000). The RSS drew inspiration from Mussolini, as we have noted. But, while engrafting Hitler's techniques on Mussolini's histrionics, it has not neglected the lucid thinking of Don Quixote.

Here, at home, its chieftain's message is simple. Christians and Muslims must 'realize their roots and Indianize themselves' (read: Hinduize themselves) (*TH* January 25, 2001). On February 24, he asked Muslims to adopt Hindu Names. 'Why can't there be a Mohammad Prasad or Mohammad Das' (*AA* February 25, 2001). Reciprocity is, of course, farthest from his mind.

Sudarshan has said a lot to invite ridicule; for instance by his theory of an explosion that destroyed the mosque. But his insistence that the minorities 'Indianize' themselves accurately reflects the central credo of the BJP and its ancestor, the Jan Sangh. In Mumbai, on September 30, 1990, in the company of Bal Thackeray, Advani, then BJP president, enthusiastically endorsed the Savarkar–Golwalkar doctrine: 'We feel that they [the minorities] must accept India as their nation and must accept the culture here.' At Ayodhya on November

19, 1990, he said, 'Henceforth only those who fight for *Hindu* interests would rule India.' On October 2, 1990, he complained that 'secular policy is putting unreasonable restrictions on Hindu aspirations.'

And what is one to make of this gem from his successor, Murli Manohar Joshi? 'Hindu *rashtra* need not be a formal structure. It is the basic culture of this country. I say that all Indian Muslims are Mohammadiya Hindus; all Indian Christians are Christi Hindus. They are Hindus who have adopted Christianity and Islam as their religion' (*SO* January 13, 1991).

Thus neither Muslims nor Christians are acceptable with distinct identities of their own. They must be Hinduized. Advani acknowledged, on March 23, 1991: 'Every nation has its heritage, culture, and in India it is what is termed as Hindu. I would like the words Hindu, Bharatiya and Indian to be synonymous.' With men such as these in power, India's secular ideology faces a 'clear and present danger.'

The BJP's allies proved a frail reed to rely on as a check on the RSS, VHP, and Bajrang Dal. They squeaked only twice. On February 2, 1999 the BJP and its allies issued a joint statement which contained four solemn resolutions. The third contained this admission: 'Since the BJP is the core of our alliance, it shall make every effort to ensure that the prestige and cohesiveness of the coalition are not diluted by *organizations belonging to its ideological fraternity*.' The myth about the Sangh *parivar*'s 'independent' bodies was exploded (*TH* February 3, 1999 for the text). On January 31 Madan Lal Khurana had held the Bajrang Dal responsible for the murder of Graham Staines and his two sons on January 22–23.

On the second occasion, December 10, 2000, the NDA even lauded Vajpayee's 'anguish' and supported him fully. Amazingly, the Prime Minister, eight union ministers, including the Home Minister, and three chief ministers, were privy to a grave factual error that 'the litigation over the title of [sic] the disputed land in Ayodhya' is before the Supreme Court whose decision the NDA promised 'to accept and implement.' The litigation, in fact, has been before the Special Bench (Ayodhya) of the Allahabad High Court at Lucknow, comprising Justices D.K. Trivedi, Syed Rafat Alam, and J.C. Mishra for the last seven years. It was transferred from the court of District Judge, Faizabad.[2]

After the 1999 elections, the allies emerged with reduced clout. If the BJP can behave as it has when it sorely needs allies in order to acquire a majority in the Lok Sabha, what will it desist from doing when it can rule on its own? 'For if they do these things in a green tree, what shall be done in the dry?' (St. Luke 23: 31).

NOTES

PREFACE

[1] Christophe Jaffrelot, *The Hindu Nationalist Movement in India, 1925 to the 1990s*, Viking 1996, p. 387.

[2] *Introduction to the Study of the Law of the Constitution*, ELBS & Macmillan, 1971, p. 80.

1 INTRODUCTION

[1] Yogendra Yadav and Sanjay Kumar, 'Interpreting the Mandate', *Frontline*, November 4, 1999.

[2] *The Brotherhood in Saffron: The Rashtriya Swayamsevak Sangh and Hindu Revivalism*, Vistaar 1987.

[3] 'Hindutva's Foreign Tie-up in the 1930s', *Economic and Political Weekly*, January 22, 2000.

[4] Many scholars of repute have documented and analysed the history of the RSS and its various fronts. Some of the more important publications include: Walter K. Andersen and Shridhar D. Damle, *The Brotherhood in Saffron*; Bruce Graham, *Hindu Nationalism and Indian Politics: The Origins and Development of the Bharatiya Jana Sangh*, Cambridge University Press 1990; Yogendra K. Malik and V.B. Singh, *Hindu Nationalist Movement in India: The Rise of the Bharatiya Janata Party*, Vistaar 1994; Christophe Jaffrelot, *The Hindu Nationalist Movement in India*; Thomas Blom Hansen, *The Saffron Wave: Democracy and Hindu Nationalism in Modern India*, Oxford University Press 1999; and Partha S. Ghosh, *BJP and the Evolution of Hindu Nationalism: From Periphery to Centre*, Manohar 1999. Reference may also be made to other useful studies: Craig Baxter, *The Jana Sangh*, University of Pennsylvania Press 1969; D.R. Goyal, *Rashtriya Swayamsevak Sangh*, Radha Krishna 1979; Nana Deshmukh, *RSS: Victim of Slander*, Vision Books 1979; Geeta Puri, *Bharatiya Jana Sangh*, Sterling 1980; K.R. Malkani, *The RSS Story*, Impex India 1980; and Dina Nath Mishra, *RSS: Myth and Reality*, Vikas 1980.

[5] *The Brotherhood in Saffron*, p. 33.

⁶ Y.D. Gundevia, *Outside the Archives*, Sangam Books 1984, p. 210.
⁷ *People's Democracy*, December 9, 1990.
⁸ *Portrait of A Martyr*, Jaico 1969, pp. 90–100.
⁹ *A Life of Our Times*, Orient Longman 1998, pp. 93–94.

2 THE RSS: OUTLOOK AND POLICIES

¹ For a thorough exposure of this, see Sitaram Yechury, *What is this Hindu Rashtra*, A Frontline Publication, 1993.
² Donald E. Smith, *India as a Secular State*, Oxford University Press 1963.
³ For the entire correspondence, see Prakash Vibhagi, *Justice on Trial: A Collection of the Historic Letters Between Shri Guruji and the Government (1948–49)*, RSS, Karnataka, 1969.
⁴ Durga Das (ed.), *Sardar Patel's Correspondence* (1945–50); *Navajivan* volume 7, p. 672.
⁵ Dhirendra Sharma (ed.), *The Janata (People's) Struggle*, A Philosophy and Social Action Publication 1977, p. 305.

3 THE SANGH PARIVAR AND THE BRITISH

¹ S.P. Mookerjee, *Leaves from a Diary*, Oxford University Press 1993, p. 179. It is a neglected book that deserves notice.
² For the complete details, see Krishnan Dubey and Venkitesh Ramakrishnan, 'Far From Heroism: The Tale of "Veer Savarkar"', *Frontline*, April 7, 1995.
³ *The History of the Indian National Congress*, Vol. II, p. 512.
⁴ Ibid., p. 513.
⁵ Ibid., p. 514.
⁶ *Quit India Movement: British Secret Documents*; edited by P.N. Chopra and S.R. Bakshi, Interprint, New Delhi 1986, p. 314.

4 THE RSS AND GANDHI

¹ This photograph has been reproduced in Sitaram Yechury, *What is this Hindu Rashtra*, A *Frontline* Publication, 1993, p. 20.
² *Collected Works of Mahatma Gandhi*, Volume 90, p. 144. All subsequent references to quotes from Gandhi are embedded in the text.
³ *The Hindu Nationalist Movement in India*, p. 72.
⁴ Vide the writer's 'The Collaborators: The Sangh *parivar* and the British', *Frontline*, December 1, 1995.
⁵ *Mahatma Gandhi: The Last Phase*, Navajivan Publishing House, Volume II, pp.439–40.
⁶ Ibid., p. 750.

5 RSS FRONT ORGANIZATIONS

¹ *Economic and Political Weekly*, December 6, 1997.
² *Making India Hindu*, edited by David Ludden, Oxford 1996, p. 42.
³ *Religious Nationalism: Hindus and Muslims in India*, Oxford 1996, pp. 3–4.
⁴ Oxford University Press 1995, pp. 97–98.
⁵ *Making India Hindu*, edited by David Ludden.
⁶ Paul R. Brass, *Theft of an Idol*, Princeton University Press 1997, p. 17. See also *Riots and Pogroms* edited by Paul R. Brass, Macmillan 1996 for a comprehensive evaluation of the Sangh

parivar's riot strategy.

[7] *Hindu Nationalist Movement in India: The Rise of the Bharatiya Janata Party*, Vistaar 1994, p. 169.

6 DEMOLITION OF THE BABRI MASJID

[1] Madhav Godbole, *Unfinished Innings*, Orient Longman 1996, p. 406.

[2] See the writer's critique in *Constitutional Questions in India*, Oxford University Press, 2000, pp. 79–84.

7 CURRENT AGENDAS

[1] Donald Eugene Smith, *India as a Secular State*, Oxford University Press 1963, p. 437.

[2] *'Vartaman* Indian *Samvidhan'* (The Present Indian Constitution) by Swami Muktanand Saraswati, published by Akhil Bharatiya Sant Samiti, Vrindavan, and Sarvodaya Satsang Ashram, Hardwar.

[3] *The Kargil War*, LeftWord Books, 1999, p. 95.

8 EPILOGUE: RETROSPECT AND PROSPECT

[1] For more details, see the writer's detailed analysis in *Frontline*, March 30, 2001.

[2] For the text of the NDA resolution, see *The Hindu*, December 11, 2000.